For Carol
with appreciation
for your many
activities for
CFUW + me

Ruth ... R. Bell

Be A *"Nice"* Girl!

A Woman's Journey in the 20th Century

Ruth M. Bell,
C.M., B.A., M.A., LL.D. (Hon. Causa)

with Andrea M. McCormick

Copyright Ruth M. Bell & Andrea McCormick Communications Inc.
ISBN 0-9736661-0-2
Design and production: Deanna Fenwick
Printed by: Motion Creative Printing, Carleton Place, Ontario
Cover Photo: Université d'Ottawa Media Production Services

Dedication

In memory of my parents,
Olive and Roy Cooper,
and Bill Rolph, Dick Bell, and Paul Cornell
for their support and encouragement along my journey.

Acknowledgements

In appreciation and gratitude to:

my mother, my first role model,

my husband, Bill, who encouraged me to undertake university studies,

my husband, Dick, and my stepdaughter, Judy, who actively supported
me and contributed to my efforts to improve the status of women,

Dr. Paul Cornell who made it possible for me to have an
academic career and who shares our octogenarian years,

Dr. Eugene Forsey who together with other
teachers enlightened my journey,

my colleagues from many lands and particularly the International
Federation of University Women, the Canadian Federation of
University Women, and the National Council of Women who shared
my journey and who suggested these memoirs be written,

Brenda Rothwell who orchestrated the initial
meeting to discuss these memoirs,

and

Andrea McCormick whose herculean labours have
brought forth this literary production.

My thanks to you all.

CONTENTS

Continued

*"Bless this food to our use
and us to thy service
and make us ever **needful** of
the **minds** of others."*

When I was a little girl, I remember my grandmother telling me how she and her mother marched for suffrage in Michigan, USA.

The quest for equality began in earnest at Seneca Falls, New York in 1848 when a group of suffragettes used the *Declaration of Independence* to highlight a litany of gender inequities in property law, education, employment, and religion. The controversy over women's radical demands—and particularly the right to vote—raged for more than half a century before the laws of the land changed. Women in Michigan were among the first female Americans to gain the vote in 1917, two years before I was born.

Canadian women mounted equally successful campaigns because they knew that without a vote, they had no voice in government and its programs and policies. Prohibition and social reforms to protect children were just some of the issues. A relentless and protracted lobby for the vote started in western Canada and moved across the country. Lobby groups, formed specifically to improve women's economic and legal status and educational opportunities, proliferated and included the Canadian Women's Suffrage Association (1883), the Dominion Women's Enfranchisement Association (1889), the National Council of Women (1893) and the University Women's Club of Ottawa (1910).

Most assuredly, men held the power. Canadian women worked together to build a powerful coalition of men and women to persuade legislators that change was necessary. After much resistance, most Canadian women became voters when the Women's Franchise Act came into force on January 1, 1919.

How was I to know the feelings of unrest I experienced earlier in life would define what I did within my sphere of influence? After all, by the time I arrived in this world, most women could vote and they had the right to seek election.

So what was the problem? The reality was—we were just beginning to reinterpret the rights and privileges accorded to men and women through law and custom. In fact, some remarkable changes to male standards and female behaviours occurred as the vestiges of 20th century power and its prejudices and privileges gave way to a more harmonious and more judicious application of the principles of equality. The famous *Persons Case* of 1929 in which five women challenged the prevailing view that women were not persons, pension reform, parental leave, property law reform, the appointments of qualified women to public and private boards, and the protection of rights of native women who married non-native men are just a few examples. In telling my story, I also will refer to some other women's achievements because their perseverance made it possible for me and my generation to go forward.

As we strive to reach the next level in this odyssey of human evolution, we do so knowing that the concrete ceiling that once blocked women's progress became a glass ceiling by the end of the 20th century.

Today, the average earnings of employed women represent about 73% of that of men. Some careers have opened up to women yet women represent only about one in five professionals employed in natural sciences, mathematics and engineering. Men are doing more to help around the house but employed women continue to carry the bulk of responsibilities in looking after their homes and families. I am not sure that raising a family with both parents in the workforce is a good idea. I don't know what the answer is to that.

Where do we go from here? Continual progress will come about—albeit slowly—if we first become familiar with the history and circumstances of an issue before we try to educate and persuade others to take action. Creating that dialogue requires us to suspend our own opinions when we are listening to others, and we have to persuade men, and women to take the time to look beyond a person's physical appearance to discover his or her essence.

We have had regressive moments if you use the reaction to Belinda Stronach's decision to seek the leadership of the new Conservative Party as a barometer. All sorts of people, including the news media, twittered about Belinda's appearance, her clothes and her shoes. You don't see the media describing a male candidate as that tall, blonde, striking fellow with bright blue eyes and spectacular suits. This is 2004. We need to hear the candidate's ideas and what he/she supports. Whether one is sexy or is a single parent is of no concern.

Diverse and divergent opinions naturally create tensions but let's not confuse that discomfort with the perils of stereotyping. How much of the Right Hon. Kim Campbell's failure to lead the PC Party to victory can be attributed to voters' inability to accept her because she was a female? Are we going to continue to marginalize women's creativity and leadership abilities or are we going to embrace them as the other half of our interconnected world?

I enjoyed being a leader and a doer. I liked being a part of something— whether it was serving as Head Girl at St. Clement's School, as a member of the faculty at the University of Waterloo or Carleton University, leading the Canadian Federation of University Women, or supporting UNESCO. I liked getting people together to make a situation better than it was. I always had people behind me or working with me to accomplish a goal within our resources. There is no point expending a lot of energy on too wide a scope. You just can't get it all done. You have to be content with what you achieve and know others will pick up where you left off. You can't stay around forever. You need new people and new ideas.

To be a leader today, in a political sense, often is a thankless job. Accolades are few and far between. It almost seems that while we don't want to take on a leadership role ourselves, we don't want anyone else to do it either. We vilify the person instead of debating the policy. How much information is intended to be benign and how much is intended to malign by creating doubts and uncertainty? Do we want our society to disintegrate into nothing but confusion? I am very worried about this trend away from sincerity and respect for one another.

Leadership is a very scarce commodity and it is a worry to me, not only nationally but internationally and in my own world—the volunteer world. Volunteering provides a means of making person-to-person contact, of restoring individualism, identity, and self-respect. Volunteering provides the means for people to move from being spectators to becoming true participants in solving community problems.

The presence of volunteer groups is a hallmark of freedom and democracy. They contribute to national unity, international understanding and fellowship. Indeed, the maintenance of democracy may well depend upon the health of the voluntary sector—upon the idea that citizens have a continuing responsibility not only to do things for themselves but also to do things for and with others.

As a head table guest, I often was asked to say Grace. My favourite was one I altered to read "Bless this food to our use and us to thy service and make us ever needful of the minds of others."

The Right Hon. Pierre Trudeau enjoyed it so much when he heard me deliver it at a joint meeting of the Canadian Clubs that he used it on a Sunday broadcast the following evening, according to the late Senator Bill Benidickson.

As you read about my journey, I hope you will reflect on the influence you can have on a person-to-person basis. Most of all, I hope it will reinforce your belief in the power of a community that pulls together. I want to make a small amendment to a closing statement in speeches I made 30 and 40 years ago:

*"If ever the world sees a time when women **and men** shall come together purely and simply for the benefit and good of mankind, it will be a power such as the world has never known."*

Ruth M. Bell, C.M.

CHAPTER ONE

My Journey Begins

Growing up

Ol' man winter came in like a lion on November 29, 1919, coating the streets of Detroit, Michigan, with heavy sheets of ice and snow. Lights flickered and then the city went dark. Surgeons at Harper Hospital were performing what was then a major abdominal procedure on my mother—a caesarean section—in an operating room, powered by a generator. I was lifted out of her womb at 6:40 p.m. Mother developed pneumonia and almost died. Daddy used to tease me about how the world changed when I was born.

Daddy wasn't permitted to visit Mother for a few days because she was so sick. When visiting was allowed, Mother managed, with help from the nurses, to put on her lipstick and make herself presentable. Daddy initially didn't care to see the baby who had caused all the trouble. "My God, I am never going through this again," he said when he finally saw my mother. When Mother was well enough to go home, Daddy hired a nurse and my first friend, Elizabeth Buck, to help her and care for me. That friendship lasted a lifetime.

Soon after my arrival, my grandmothers came to call—one from St. Thomas, Ontario and the other from Flint, Michigan. My mother's mother thought I should be called *Royetta* because I looked so much like my father. Thank heavens that idea didn't carry the day! They settled on Ruth Marion Cooper.

My mother, Olive Pearl O'Mulvenny, was a small woman who had a beautiful voice and loved to play the piano. Mother was a native of Hagersville. Before she married, she taught school in the Huntsville area.

Daddy was born in Cheboygan, Michigan and grew up in Flint, Michigan, an automotive industrial centre. He was selling automotive parts when he

Olive Pearl O'Mulvenny

and Mother met in Detroit. How Mother got to Detroit, I am not certain. I can only guess that Mother was taking music lessons. I do know Mother sang at many places of worship including a Jewish synagogue. Mother changed her religion from Methodist to Episcopalian when she married Daddy, and they always took me to Sunday school and to church on high days and holy days.

Roy Lawrence Cooper

Mother introduced me to music and took me to concerts where I listened to performers such as tenor Enrico Caruso, violinist Fritz Kreisler, and Paul Robeson, one of the most popular concert singers of his time and known for his trademark Ol' Man River. I still have an autographed program of Paul's.

I absolutely adored my father. Daddy gave me an irreplaceable gift at an early age—a love of books. He read to me and encouraged me to read by giving me what were almost indestructible children's classics made from rag-cloth. *Uncle Wiggly* was my first book. Daddy taught me how to play cards. By the time I was eight, I played bridge, cribbage and solitaire, but he drew the line at poker. I learned that game later in life on my return by freighter from Australia. Daddy encouraged me to learn to swim and to play tennis and golf. I don't remember if he was a sports fan, but I do remember him taking me to the golf course and making me swat a few balls.

These gifts from my parents have been a source of education and pleasure throughout my life.

The earliest childhood story I was told was about my first encounter with Santa. When I was two or three, Daddy was delegated to take me to the local department store to see the jolly fellow with the white beard. Daddy and I watched the children as they sat on Santa's knee and listened to Santa's questions. When it was my turn, I was ready. Apparently, I was hard to miss. My flaming red hair, which tumbled out of my hood, was matched by my very loud voice.

"What is your name, and have you been a good girl, and what do you want me to bring you for Christmas?" the kind Santa asked.

According to Daddy, I raced through my answer: "My name is Ruthie Cooper; I have been a good girl and I clean up my plate and I don't pee-pee my pants and I want a Mama doll."

I was quite young when I discovered the difference between boys and girls. We were living on Euclid Avenue in Detroit. The little boy who lived next door and I were playing in the sandbox Daddy had built for me. Mother took my clothes off and sprinkled me and my friend, who was also in his birthday suit, with a hose because it was such a hot, summer day. I noticed something was quite different. When it was time for supper, I ran into the house, sobbing along the way. My limited vocabulary made it difficult to describe the cause of my anguish so I resorted to making up a new word.

"I want a tostle just like Johnnie has," I wailed as I ran to Mother. I had never seen a tostle (tassel) before because I had no brothers. From that day on, I always wished I were a boy.

Daddy insisted I attend a private school because he didn't think much of the public school system. Mother kept it up when we moved to Canada. My earliest recollection was boarding at Miss Aiken's Open Air School for Girls in St. Petersburg, Florida while my parents vacationed in Cuba. When my father's automotive parts business took us to Atlanta, Georgia, I attended North Avenue Presbyterian School—a Christian school that included bible studies in its curriculum. I still have the bible. I won a gold medal as the top speller in the lower grades because my father insisted on teaching me how to spell. We were very pleased with the medal.

I am not sure whether I was bad or clever as a child. I recall one incident when I was about seven or eight. My parents were having a dinner party and they asked me to sit at the table with the guests. So I did. I had my dinner, and apparently I was well-behaved. The guests continued to visit after I was sent to bed. Somewhere along the line, I called out, "Daddy, bring me a drink of water."

He didn't reply. I ask for water two or three times before he finally said, "Shut up and go to sleep."

"Daddy, I want a drink of water!"

"If you don't shut up, I am going to come in there and spank you," he warned.

"Well, on your way in, would you please bring me a drink of water?" came the precocious reply.

The first Christmas I can recall was at our home at 145 East Lake Drive in Atlanta. It was a large, white brick house. All of our bedrooms, the living room and the dining room had fireplaces. Behind the living room was a study where Daddy kept his business papers and a bookcase jammed with books. A hand-lettered sign reading "Bear's Den. Stay Out!" was displayed prominently on the door. I was allowed in only when Daddy was in the study.

One day, Mother asked me to answer the door. Two men brought in a very large box which Mother directed into the study. A day or two later when she wasn't around, I sneaked into the study and found a lovely desk. I thought it rather strange that Daddy would want a desk with little drawers and a sliding shelf. It was a big mystery to me! I began to play office, filling the little drawers with Sears' money and my father's well-sharpened pencils, that is until Mother ordered me out and up to my room.

I rose early Christmas morning and was given permission to run downstairs to the living room where there was an enormous tree, beautifully decorated with red, green, silver and gold ropes, and a pink spire at the top. That spire remained in the Christmas decorating box until after my mother died 30 years later. Several birds with shiny, soft tails were clipped onto the branches. In front of the tree, I saw a white doll's bed and a large girl-doll in a dress. "Betty's" real hair was adorned with a ribbon, and she wore socks and black patent slippers just like mine. A doll's trunk was open and clothing was draped from the drawers. There was the desk and right on the front of the desk was a card, in my father's distinctive handwriting, addressed to Ruth Cooper from Santa. When I asked him how the desk came down the little chimney and why it looked like the desk in the study, Daddy told me Santa had asked him to help him. Daddy assured me Santa had enjoyed the chocolate cake, which was my

Dad's favourite, and the glass of milk. My lurking suspicions soon were forgotten with the busyness of dressing and undressing Betty and introducing her to my bear, Teddy, and my baby doll, Royal, who was named after the baking powder Mother used.

Mother and I had a meeting of the minds one day over a milk glass ornament. Mother loved to visit antique shops, and sometimes I had to go with her. I was told to be a good girl and to sit quietly in the shop, a situation which I found very boring. One day, I spotted a milk glass hen that I wanted, but Mother refused to give me the 25 cents to pay for it. We left the shop without it.

Shortly after, Grandma Margaret from St. Thomas came to Atlanta to celebrate my mother's birthday. Grandma asked me if I knew of anything Mother wanted for her birthday. I said yes, with glee! Grandma and I got on the streetcar and went to the antique shop. I am amazed I knew how to get there. I showed her the hen with the red wax eyes. Now, Grandma couldn't understand why Mother hadn't bought it if she had wanted it because it was only 25 cents.

The coveted hen with the red wax eyes is displayed prominently in my curio cabinet today.

"I don't know why she didn't buy it but she really would like it," I assured Grandma.

Grandma bought the hen and, for an extra 50 cents, a plate to set underneath it. The gift was wrapped and given to Mother. Mother opened the present. She looked at the hen and then she looked at me. I can still see her face. I was absolutely petrified at the thought of what she might say. She didn't say anything rude, choosing instead to thank Grandma for the thoughtful gift. After Grandma left, Mother was quick to give me a scolding. "What the heck did you do that for? You know, I don't want this hen."

I was nine when we moved to a new, larger house on a hill on Morningside Drive in Atlanta. It had a large living room, sunroom, dining room and kitchen on the main floor. Daddy's office was upstairs in a room that was lined with books. Under the window was a fine couch where I read everything I could including the *Bobbsey Twins* and all the Elsie Dinsmore books. Naturally, I couldn't keep any of them because they belonged to the house.

Lizzie was hired to look after me and the house. She was a grand cook who made scrumptious fried pies as well as grits and greens, and she was a great whistler. Lizzie and her husband, Gus, lived in a small house at the back. Gus was as thin and wiry and small as Lizzie was plump and large. Gus drove me to and from school and tended the furnace and the garden.

It was here that I had my first kitten. She adopted us and I loved that kitten dearly. Mother and Lizzie didn't want to keep the kitten because it was dirty. I wasn't very good at cleaning up after it, so it was sent away.

That Christmas I had been quite sick with a fever. I seem to think I had double mastoiditis and was away from school for several weeks. Daddy bundled me up in blankets and brought me downstairs to the living room to join a flu-stricken Gus. There sat Gus, wrapped in blankets and wearing his battered old hat on his head. A bare tree stood in the sunroom and colourful parcels were heaped on the piano. Daddy started to put lights, which were a new invention, on the Christmas tree but not before he sought our advice on colour and location. I can still hear Gus saying, "Ah don't care what colour it is, so long as it is red."

That was the year I received Mary Mapes Dodge's *Hans Brinker or the Silver Skates* and Hawthorne's *Wonderbook of Tanglewood Tales*. In the midst of all the brightly wrapped parcels was an old, charcoal sack tied up with a red ribbon. It was for Mother from Santa. She opened it gingerly and unwrapped several layers of paper to reveal her heart's desire: an amethyst dinner ring. That was the year I was pretty sure Daddy was more than just a helper to Santa.

A week before Christmas of 1929, my beloved Daddy died suddenly. He was 40. I was 10. It was a very sad time. I suffered with a stomach ailment for several years after. I eventually got over that, but his death continued to upset me for years because I was so very partial to him and I knew he loved me dearly. I felt so alone. That feeling would haunt me for most of my life.

Mother was left to raise me. It was hard for her because she had hardly any money. Mother had to go out to work at a time when mothers didn't work— at least at our level of society—because the insurance policies Daddy left us weren't enough to cover our living expenses. Mother had to decide whether to redeem my policy at its face value of $5,000 or take an annual income of $199 per year. Mother chose the latter and I still receive a cheque today.

We moved out of our big new house, which my parents had bought just months earlier, to an apartment. In the summer of 1931, Mother decided to get a job and move to Toronto where she had family so that I would not be alone if something happened to her. We had no relatives in Atlanta. As a widow, Mother appreciated the importance of insurance as a contingency to deal with life's unexpected blows. Her personal experience influenced her decision to become a certified insurance agent and enter the tough world of selling for Canada Life in Toronto.

Our apartment was close to my new school, St. Clement's, a private Anglican girls' school. I spent my last year of primary school and five years of high school at St. Clement's. My father's eldest sister, Florence, was not at all impressed that Mother had to work, and her family thought Mother extravagant for continuing my education at a private school.

Mother chose St. Clement's for two reasons. The school would keep me until 5 p.m. if Mother had a late afternoon business appointment. As important, it would be cheaper for me to attend a private school because I would have to wear a school uniform. That would solve the financial problem we would face had I attended a public school—where the competition among girls for cashmere sweaters and saddle-shoes was fierce even during the dark days of the Great Depression. Typically, a girl's clothing allowance was between $20 and $25 a month. Mine was $1 a week. I had two school uniforms in that six-year period. My weekend wardrobe consisted of a skirt and shirt, a dress and a party dress. We didn't change our clothes every day.

As a non-Canadian, I was quite noticeable especially with my American accent, but I got along well with my classmates. My friends liked to visit me because I lived in an apartment which was very different from their homes. We always had cookies and something nice to drink. When Mother was there, she would visit with us.

Mothers were either scornful of my working mother or they felt sorry for me and often invited me to their cottages. Mother found selling insurance very difficult, but it was far better than a 9-to-5 job. Her time was her own. If she had something she had to do with me, she could. She wasn't paid by the hour or the day. She was paid a commission on what she sold. Quite often, she worked at home on the telephone. As I recall, she found it very difficult to make a "cold call." Most of the prospective clients were men. Not many women made their living in the financial world or made decisions on investments, but she believed in what she was doing—making sure families had adequate insurance to meet their needs.

At the time, women's choices were quite limited. It may be hard for younger people today to understand the attitudes women faced then. For example, it wasn't until 1919 that most Canadian women were given the right to vote and to register as candidates in federal elections. Up until 1929, the popular interpretation of the British North America Act suggested women were not persons and therefore weren't qualified to be appointed to the Senate. Women have worked hard over the last century to improve the status of women and quality of life. We take our right to be active in public office as an elected or appointed official for granted now, but it wasn't always that way.

I remember, very well, the day Mother was entertaining some women. They were talking about a friend who just had a baby. I was in the other room when I heard about the woman's dreadful, agonizing experience, and how they hoped she would regain her health. Up to this point in my life, all I knew was what Mother had told me: I had slept under her heart for nine months. Mother realized I had overhead the conversation and decided to tell me about babies and where they came from. She phrased it very beautifully. I can still remember the conversation. She told me what happened and how the baby came into the world. I didn't believe her, so I went upstairs, got a mirror and looked. I couldn't see how any baby could come out of there. For a long time, I just thought Mother was telling me nice stories when in fact, she had told me the truth.

Mother dispensed advice at different times of my life. I recall one incident in my early teens. A man Mother knew promised to give me a watch if I came down to his office. I wanted a watch in the worst way. When I told her, Mother cautioned me by saying, "You go down, but remember, if he is going to give you a watch, he is going to want something in return. If he tries to get fresh with you, just swat him in the face and walk away! Be prepared for that because he is not going to give you a watch just because he is being generous!"

So, I got all dressed up and went to the office. Sure enough, he wanted to have a little familiarity, so I did exactly what my mother told me to do. I swatted him across the face and walked out. I did not get the watch. In fact, I didn't own a watch until I was married.

Mother arranged for a friend to have a private conversation with me. This very nice gentleman warned me about men who might try to touch my private parts or who would try to have sex with me without my consent.

"You just have to be firm. Don't try to be liked by everyone because some people are just after you for what they can get in the way of sex," he warned. He showed me how to use the knee—a technique I successfully applied later in my youth! As I recall, I had agreed to go out with a friend of a friend of mine to a supper dance at the Royal York, which was the thing to do then. I very foolishly went with him up to his room. I never thought anything more about it. Needless to say, he got a little familiar, so I couldn't do anything about it except to use my knee. While he was writhing on the floor, I picked up my purse and went out to the street to board a streetcar. It was 10 or 11 at night. I had no money to board a streetcar so I hailed a taxi. When I arrived home, the driver waited while I went into the house to get some money from my mother. That's how she found out about it. When I told her what I had done, she was quite pleased with me.

Mother would not tolerate bigotry during a time when bigotry was quite common. I know because I experienced it. My friend, Margaret, and her mother, who was also a widow, lived in our building. Margaret went to a Catholic school across the street from us. Our school friends criticized our friendship on religious grounds. At St. Clement's, some students weren't Anglicans but there were no Catholics. In those days, Laura Secord would hire only Roman Catholics as clerks and other businesses would hire only Protestants. During that era, Jewish people could not join the Granite Club, and they weren't allowed at some resorts. There was almost as much discrimination against Protestants and Catholics as there was against Jews. Most assuredly, at that time not many of us knew the extent of the Holocaust during the Second World War. Perhaps the Government did, but it was not common knowledge that six million Jews were being murdered.

Mother insisted we attend a Catholic Church on Good Friday for the *Stations of the Cross*—a commemoration of 14 events beginning with the condemnation of Jesus and ending with His burial in a tomb. We also had Jewish friends—the Josephs—who invited us to Jewish High Holiday observance services such as *Yom Kippur*—the Day of Atonement and the most solemn day of the Jewish calendar. I called him, *Uncle* Ken and her, *Aunt* Pauline. Their son, Monte, attended medical school when I was in high school. He introduced me to many books and took me to university dances which I enjoyed tremendously. A worried Uncle Ken came to see Mother because he was very concerned Monte and I would want to be married.

"What if they do?" Mother asked.

"It would be dreadful because he would be ostracized by the Jewish community and she would be ostracized by the Gentile community. In the Jewish faith, it is the mother who must raise the children according to our religion," he explained.

"I don't think they are thinking of getting married. They would have nothing to live on," she replied.

Monte became a psychiatrist and practised in the United States. He married a French Canadian, Roman Catholic nurse. The Josephs' daughter, Erica, married a Jewish boy and the marriage didn't work out.

I wouldn't say I was bigoted or my mother was bigoted. But generally, you moved in your own religious circles. It may be hard to understand that attitude today because there is a greater acceptance of religious differences.

I certainly had to be independent. One year, many of my teenaged friends were going to work as waitresses at summer resorts. Mother would not allow me to go because she had heard all kinds of stories about girls getting pregnant. In those days, if a girl got in the family way, it was a disgrace for the whole family.

Instead, my friend Doris Chappell and I volunteered to be counselors at a camp for children who had been exposed to tuberculosis (TB). For Doris and me, it was just like going to a resort. Most of the children came from poor families where one or more family members suffered from this chronic, bacterial lung disease. The incidence of TB eventually decreased in the 1940s and 1950s, once an effective antibiotic therapy was developed. In the interim, summer camps provided children with two to three weeks of sunshine and good food.

Another summer, my mother gave me the weekly household money and insisted I manage the house. The housekeeper, who was paid $1 a day, was dismissed for the duration. Mother reasoned that if I were to marry a rich man, I would know how to handle the servants; if I were to marry a poor man, I would know how to run the house. Cooking was part of the initiation. We ate tomato aspic every day for a week because I didn't know how to adjust the recipe to two servings.

University: A dream dashed

Looking back, Mother was very strict—in some ways harsh. She insisted I stand first in class which I did until fifth form—my last year of high school. I was very good in languages and studied Latin, English, French, German and Spanish as well as mathematics and history. My dream was to go to university to study languages.

I was Head Girl during fifth form. I was very happy and my mother was very proud of me because I had been chosen by the teachers. They outvoted the principal. Head girl carried some responsibilities—in this case, overseeing school discipline. If a teacher were late, I would be the substitute until she arrived. If a student wore lipstick to school, I or a prefect would take her into the washroom and wash her face with soap. That year, I also met my first serious beau, and we were very partial to each other. Between my responsibilities, the books and the beau, I stood second in class for the first time ever. That meant there would be no scholarship and without a scholarship, I wouldn't be going to university.

I was Head Girl in the St. Clement's Graduating Class of 1937-1938.

Mother responded by returning the gift she had purchased for me and the gifts sent by friends. To make matters worse, the school principal insisted I was not "university material." While I can't prove it, I suspect my mother had encouraged the principal to discourage me from attending university. Sufficient money was left by my father to pay for my university fees but there was not enough to cover room and board.

I didn't receive a scholarship but I did receive the highest honour St. Clement's could bestow when I graduated in 1938: the Powell Memorial Prize. The prize was the *Oxford Book of English Verse*, a book I love dearly to this day.

Some of my friends, many of whom were debutantes, went on to university.

My second husband, Dick Bell, used to think I was very self-sufficient. He called me a survivor. His daughter, Judy, thought I was the most stubborn, persistent woman she had ever met because anything I started, I was determined to complete it. I think I got that trait from my mother.

Since my grades weren't good enough to earn a scholarship, I entered the work force at the age of 18. That didn't dampen my desire to obtain a university education. I just didn't know where to start because I had no connections. Advisory services for young people didn't exist so you had to find things out for yourself. Luckily, the father of one of my friends took me in hand and helped me in many ways.

Initially, I worked half-days as a clerk for our family physician, Dr. Brown, Mondays through Fridays and Saturdays for $5 a week. In the mornings, I attended business school to learn typing, shorthand, bookkeeping and other office skills. When World War II broke out in 1939, I was working for the United States Consulate General in Toronto where I made much more money— $17.50 per week—as an immigration clerk conducting interviews and issuing visas to those eligible to migrate to the United States.

Wartime required strict adherence to immigration laws and regulations, and a quota system. Refugees from European countries such as Poland were flooding into Canada. Some refugees, who wanted to join relatives in the States, came through the U.S. Consulate. When war broke out between Finland and the Union of Soviet Socialist Republics, Finnish men from Northern Ontario applied for transit visas to board ships departing from the States to return to Finland and fight for their country. We often issued visas to Norwegians who had set up aviation training bases at Toronto Island and in the Muskokas in Ontario shortly after their country was invaded. I have kept a memento of those times—a sterling silver pin I was given at a dinner party hosted by Norwegian aviators.

It was thrilling to issue temporary visas to movie stars such as Vivian Leigh and Lawrence Olivier who were entering the States to pursue their careers. Then, there were the von Trapp singers whose story of flight after Hitler's Nazis invaded Austria inspired the movie *The Sound of Music* with Julie Andrews and Christopher Plummer. Maria and George and the seven von Trapp children entertained us with their lovely music as they applied for visas at the U.S. Consulate. They eventually settled in Vermont.

I interviewed a great many Jews who had escaped from Poland and Eastern Europe and who were very relieved to get out. Some families were accompanied by a translator who would translate English to Yiddish. One family from Krakow, Poland crossed Siberia and came to Canada by way of Japan. Immigration into the United States was limited, so they either stayed in Canada or waited until immigration opened up.

At the time, I experienced feelings of great admiration and fear as I learned, through the interviews, what some of the human race was going through just because they happened to be Jewish. Many of us did not yet know about the atrocities committed at concentration camps. I heard many stories of great upheaval and disruption. One family had been incarcerated in an attic in the Netherlands until their escape could be arranged. Others fled with only the jewellery and money they could sew into their clothes. Those who didn't have money or connections weren't so lucky. I recall feeling glad that I lived in Canada after I thought about what would have happened to me and my mother had we lived under those circumstances. We had no connections.

The name of the person you would interview was determined by a draw which is how I came to interview my first husband William (Bill) Rolph who was applying for a visa to do postgraduate work in Providence, Rhode Island, in 1941.

Destiny or serendipity: My courtship with Bill

Was it serendipitous when I drew Bill's name to interview at the U.S. Consulate? I recognized Bill as the young man from a previous incident during my days at St. Clement's. I was traveling downtown by streetcar. Several boys were sitting on the bench across from me. One fellow was holding forth, in a loud voice, talking about the American Civil War, the generals and the many battles. As an American, I was absolutely fascinated. I was tempted to speak to him when we got off at the same stop, but I was too shy. I just knew he was an American fellow living in Toronto.

Before I started the interview, I shared my recollection of the streetcar soliloquy with him. We began to chat away. By the time I finished, I knew about his high school, where he lived and his hobbies, all of which you would ask as part of the interview. As it turned out, he wasn't an American. His family lived in Toronto; he was an avid reader of history; and his hobby was the American Civil War.

During the interview, I learned Bill had decided to pursue his postgraduate education after the Canadian army refused to enlist him for medical reasons. That must have been disappointing for Bill because he had prepared to serve by enrolling in the Canadian Officers Training Corps' military program at university.

The next week, my mother and I were going to Boston by bus. I needed to return some library books before we left. I literally collided with Bill at the

Bill Rolph and his parents W. Frank and Amanda (Maidie) Rolph

library. He was working in a nearby office for the summer. As we started to talk, he offered to escort me home. Bill thought I still lived in north Toronto and I thought he had a car, neither of which was true. He accompanied me on the streetcar to my home in another part of the city.

As chance would have it, we discovered we were going to be in New England at the same time which prompted Bill to invite me to dinner in Boston. Much to my mother's annoyance, we kept the date. She didn't approve of me going out with him because she didn't know anything about him. His parents didn't approve either because they didn't know my family. In those days, I guess, we were much more careful with our young people.

We went to dinner and we corresponded a bit while he was away at university. We spent time together the next summer before he returned to Rhode Island to continue his postgraduate work. Before his studies were completed, Bill was employed by the Wartime Information Office in Ottawa. He received a conscription notice, only to be rejected, once again, for medical reasons. Bill went on to teach at the University of Western Ontario.

I continued to work at the U.S. Consulate and quite enjoyed the variety of work. I had to know the law and the regulations, and how to interpret them. At the same time, I realized my future was limited. You needed a degree to be an officer and there were no women in officer positions. Work was a financial necessity for me. The answer was to take university courses in the evening at the University of Toronto and work during the day. When I investigated that option, I discovered the university only offered credit courses during the day and non-credit adult education courses in the evening. That made it impossible for me to pursue a degree and work at the same time. Now, I knew my future was limited here, but I didn't know just how limited. Here's what happened.

BE A "*NICE*" GIRL!

A mother's advice:
"Stand up for your rights!"

My first exposure to discrimination occurred at the U.S. Consulate after a trade and commerce officer requested my help. I soon discovered why. When I told Mother he liked to chase me around the desk, she said: "Stand up for your rights!" When I did, I was fired, allegedly because I was an uncooperative worker which really meant I wouldn't let him get familiar with me.

It was always the girl's fault. However, I knew the regulations. I was entitled to six months' pay and relocation costs. I received compensation for keeping my mouth shut. Years later, this man was dismissed because of similar complaints.

I always thought I would enjoy traveling which is what prompted me to apply for a teaching position at Pan American Airways at LaGuardia International. In those days, Pan American flew Boeing 315s during the summer to: Moncton, N.B.; Botwood, Nfld.; and Shannon, Ireland. Newfoundland had yet to become a part of Canada. In the winter, the airline flew to: Hamilton Harbour, Bermuda; Lisbon, Portugal; and Dakar, French West Africa.

The knowledge and experience I gained at the U.S. Consulate General were invaluable because I was hired to teach staff about the intricacies of customs and immigration laws and regulations. Staff would be deployed to other locations around the world and it would be their responsibility to determine each passenger's eligibility to enter the United States, before the ticket was issued. Otherwise, the airline was obliged to return the passenger to his/her point of origin at the airline's expense should entry to the U.S. be denied. Mother accompanied me to New York to help me get settled in the spring of 1944. Unfortunately, I didn't get to travel as much as I had hoped because of the war.

All the while, the relationship with Bill was an on-again, off-again, home-again, Flannigan relationship. When he was in Providence, Rhode Island, I was in Toronto. While I was in New York, my mother came to visit me to tell me some stories about Bill that I didn't like. I reacted by breaking up with him. To my great dismay, I discovered later that my mother had not told me the truth. By then, he was teaching history at the University of Western Ontario in London. I telephoned him to apologize.

"I just learned that what I had been told was not the case. I know it is too late to do anything about it, but I want you to know how very, very, sorry I am," I said.

"I will come down next weekend," he replied. When he arrived, Bill brought an engagement ring with him.

Bill had wonderful blue eyes. He had a good sense of humour; he was lots of fun and he loved to do things. He was a hard worker and a hard player. If I ever had cause for jealousy, it would be his friends. Bill was very, very partial to his friends. They came second, after me. He kept in touch with them all his life. I received wonderful letters from them after he died. I maintained contact with three of his students and occasionally have lunch with two who live here. One became vice-president of Trent University and the other was a Foreign Service officer to various countries. The third, now deceased, was also a Foreign Service officer.

Bill and I were to be married in New York City. Mother was so upset about our engagement that she refused to attend the wedding. Mother believed Bill wasn't going to be in a position to help support her which was why she wanted me to marry another man whose father was a millionaire. Bill had a poor health record and often suffered from migraines. He wasn't wealthy either. She was worrying about her own future—something I didn't realize, until later.

Bill's uncle and aunt, John and Dorothy Rolph, lived in New York and were very fond of Bill. With no children of their own, they regarded him as a son. They were only too happy to make the wedding arrangements for us.

Our attendants and Bill's parents, W. Frank Rolph and Amanda (Maidie), were going to travel to New York from Toronto. Maidie was a bouncy, little lady who was very enthusiastic and interested in all sorts of things. Bill and his mother were quite outgoing. Frank, a bank manager, was a very quiet man, and a very supportive guy who was extremely proud of his son.

About 10 days before the ceremony, Mother telephoned to ask me to call off the wedding. I refused.

"Well, you better come home and get married because you are only going to get married once," she conceded. "You might as well do it properly."

"All right, but you will have to make all the arrangements because I don't have time," I countered.

I telephoned Bill and he agreed with the new plan. William Kirby Rolph and I were married at Toronto's Grace Church-on-the-Hill on September 5, 1945. We went to Boston for our honeymoon because that was where we had our first date.

On our way back, I stopped off at Mother's home in Toronto to pack up our wedding gifts. Mother gave me other things from her home that she thought I would like. That's when I told her I really wanted the hen that my grandmother had bought Mother years earlier, at my insistence.

"No," she said. "My mother gave me the hen for my birthday and I am not going to give it to you." I pleaded with her, but to no avail.

She not only refused to give me the hen, she also presented me with a piece of paper listing the expenses she had incurred to raise me. It came to $10,000.

Bill and I were married at Toronto's Grace Church-on-the-Hill.

"That's what it cost me to raise you and I expect to be re-imbursed," she declared.

"Mother, you will have a long wait, because I don't have that kind of money and I don't know if I ever will."

I think she presented me with the bill because of her financial insecurity. I remember her calling me, years later, to tell me she wanted to fulfill a dream of hers—a trip to South America, but she was hesitant. She was worried that if she took the trip, she wouldn't have much money to leave me.

"Well Mother, I think you have given me enough. Don't worry about leaving me any money. If you want to go on that trip and it is something you have dreamed about, go."

So she went.

"Mrs. Rolph, which university did you attend?"

For the next two years, Bill and I made our home in London, Ontario. Bill taught at the university and I worked in the university library. Living on an instructor's salary left little for concerts or books so the 50 cents an hour I earned helped to cover the costs of those pleasures. As the newcomer, I was invited to a faculty wives' function. En route by car, each woman pointedly identified the university she had attended. One turned to me and asked, "Mrs. Rolph, which university did you attend?"

"St. Clement's," I quickly replied, thinking they wouldn't know where St. Clement's was or whether or not it was a university. But I do remember feeling so ashamed that Bill had married this uneducated female. I didn't want to embarrass my husband. I was so mortified that I started taking university courses at Western. Sadly, when it came time to take the examinations, I was disqualified because my husband was a faculty member.

Bill often invited some of his history students to our home where we settled the affairs of the world. I had to feed these young students. I was just a young bride and I didn't know much about cooking, but I could bake raspberry tarts. Don Eldon, John Harrington, Jim Johnston, Jim Gillies and Ted Galpin were among the students. Don Eldon, a lifelong friend, recalls those meetings.

> "My first contact with Ruth was when she was Ruth Rolph, the wife of a professor at the University of Western Ontario. I was a history major. Bill Rolph was a young professor, fairly new to the University, and taught history.

> "Bill was very kind to the history majors, even though it was a large class with theologians. His interest was in politics and history, not theology. Some of us, who were history or political science majors, were invited to the Rolphs' home. Of course, Ruth was a new faculty wife. She had a job in the library where you could see her frequently waiting on students who were borrowing books.

"The sessions at Bill and Ruth's home on Central Avenue in London were fairly frequent and very enjoyable and stimulating. I had no connection whatsoever with American politics but it was a subject that greatly interested Bill. There were about six or eight of us who also enjoyed Ruth's raspberry tarts. That was my first impression of Ruth as a hostess. She was gracious, convivial and vibrant and she joined in the discussions. She was not a retiring faculty wife. Bill and Ruth were friends.

"Bill was in a department of about half a dozen history professors. Dr. Arthur Dorland was the head of the department. He was a Quaker and had an Irish wife. There was Hartley Thomas. The Chief Librarian, Fred Landon, also taught a course on Negro slavery. Jimmy Tallman taught a course in Latin American history. Bill came into this group which was already well-established.

"The Department was a congenial one. The University was much smaller, and veterans were just starting to return to university as a result of support from the Department of Veterans' Affairs. The veterans were generally a little older with a very different perspective on life. Some would be as old as or older than Bill.

"This was the type of mix. I imagine Ruth would find the faculty wives difficult, much more difficult than the men. At that time, women professors had a hard time.

Women would probably not be considered for the head of a department. Some of these professors were very highly regarded later. I don't think it was a woman's world. I have a strong impression that there was a pecking order in the faculty wives. Ruth would come in as the lowest one on the totem pole at the time. Walter Balderston, who came in later, would be of some comfort to Ruth and Bill.

"Ruth worked in the library which I imagine was more welcoming. Ruth is the type of person who is adaptable, innovative and when she has to be, philosophical. This set the basis for later contact with the Rolphs and Ruth herself."

Learning to appreciate that dreadful dirty stuff called politics

Life was about to change for both Bill and me. Fewer professors were needed at Western because enrolment, once overflowing with returning war veterans who were entitled to postsecondary education and other benefits, was easing up. That's why my husband applied for a teaching position at New York University (NYU). We lived in a very modest apartment on Long Island and took a daily 90-minute subway ride to and from the university at Washington Square in Greenwich Village. While Bill taught American history, Renaissance and Reformation history from 1947 to 1951, I worked, during the day, as the admissions clerk and secretary to the Dean at NYU's Graduate School of Retailing which entitled me to free tuition. Four nights a week, I attended NYU's Washington Square College of Arts and Science to study for a degree in languages because I wanted to become an interpreter with the United Nations. But that plan changed when I met a woman professor at NYU.

The professor absolutely fascinated me. Her name was Rita Nealon. I was in touch with her until the day she died. Certain courses were required and the others were electives. Before I could enrol in modern languages and history, I was required to take mathematics, political science, economics and other unrelated and what I thought were incomprehensible subjects. I didn't want to take political science at first because I didn't like politics. I thought it was dreadful, dirty stuff. Bill was highly amused because he was a political historian. I tried everything to get out of taking the course, but couldn't.

Rita Nealon was a woman of portly proportions; the first time I saw her enter the classroom, she literally sailed in with her enormous hat on her head. I thought, egad, what's this? Initially, I didn't like her and I didn't like the way she looked. But she was so fascinating, so realistic, and so practical that I took every political science course she offered and ultimately, I changed my field of study to political science and economics. I completed the equivalent of the third year of an under-graduate program at NYU. Rita and I became friends for life.

Through Rita, I learned an important lesson. I used to tell my students to keep an open mind. Try everything you possibly can because you never know where the penny is going to drop. I still think that is true.

When NYU acquired additional property at Washington Square North, we moved to a very nice, first floor apartment in a Georgian-style building constructed circa 1840.

It wasn't until Bill and I were living in Washington Square that we had the pleasure of enjoying a tabby named Spinnenkop—meaning "burrs in the head." Spinny was owned by a Dutch woman. When he was allowed out, Spinny came to our window to visit. We would let him in to feed him. He also drank a lot. We often looked after him when his mother went away. I still have the plant rooters she gave us which she called "knack-knicks." She always complained that we didn't have enough "knack-knicks" in our apartment. That certainly isn't true today as I have plenty of knick-knacks.

Spinnenkop

Bill was working on his thesis. As Bill's contract neared its end, he accepted a one-year appointment at the University of Saskatchewan to replace Hilda Neatby who had agreed to chair a famous commission on education. I continued working and studying at NYU. I was thrilled to make the Dean's List in February and in June of 1951 having attained an average of over 90%. I received the Evening Alumni Award for Scholarship Character and Service to the College at its 120th NYU commencement ceremonies. It is a gold medal which I treasure.

When he returned from Saskatchewan in the summer of 1951, Bill, like so many other young professors, found himself without a job. With the help of the Dean who employed me, Bill was hired at Abraham and Strauss, a department store in Brooklyn. He certainly was helpful as a sales clerk but he didn't want to make a career out of retailing. Fortunately that autumn, Bill was awarded a Ford Foundation teaching fellowship at Tulane University in New Orleans, Louisiana. Ford Foundation made an astute decision by introducing fellowships as a way to retain professors until university enrolment inevitably increased.

Washington Square Mews was my home when I pursued graduate studies at New York University. (Photo by Dorothy Rolph)

I was registered as a student in the fall term at NYU when Bill was appointed to teach at Tulane in October. We decided, that once again, I would stay behind to continue working and studying. I loved studying.

Life ran smoothly for several months until I received a telephone call from New Orleans just before Christmas. Bill's ulcers sent him to the hospital. I rushed to Bill's side immediately. When he recovered, he came back with me to pack up our apartment in New York and I moved to New Orleans with him. Shortly after I arrived in New Orleans, Bill brought a kitten home to our comfortable and spacious apartment in the Vieux Carré (French Quarter). He explained that it had followed him home.

Bill resumed his teaching, and I attended Tulane on a full-time basis between January and May of 1952 as the only female student in geology and one of two females in politics. I also studied literature. We enjoyed French cuisine at Galatoire's, Commander's and Arnaud's. The tree-lined streets, colourful flowers and spacious homes added much to the beauty and romance of New Orleans which was marred only by its rather poor system of garbage collection and its many bugs.

CHAPTER TWO

During our time in Australia, we visited Sydney and Brisbane, stayed at a sheep station and toured a number of smaller centres in New South Wales including a nature reserve in northern Queensland.

Changing Courses...

An adventure together across the oceans

By July, a new adventure was about to begin. I will remember it as the best of times and the worst of times.

We headed north to say good-bye to family and friends before beginning a six-week voyage to Australia where Bill was to become a research fellow at the new Australian National University in Canberra. When Bill's thesis was noticed by Sir Douglas Copeland, the Australian High Commissioner to Canada who became Vice-Chancellor of the new university, Bill was offered a five-year research fellowship to study the Australian Country Party. Bill's thesis was based on the social philosophy of *Henry Wise Wood*, an American resident in Alberta and president of the United Farmers of Alberta. Henry Wise Wood had been published in 1950 by the University of Toronto Press and the Oxford University Press—which was quite an honour at the time. That thesis would come into play, once again, later in my life.

The most exciting adventure of our voyage by British freighter—the M.V *City of Bath*—to Sydney, Australia was the seven-hour trip through the Panama Canal. The Captain explained the canal's operation as we stood on the deck. The freighter was raised 79 feet, passed through Gatun Lake, and descended 72 feet to the Pacific. We steamed past Balboa with great reluctance, for that was the last bit of land we saw for 23 days. The Pacific was neither blue, nor beautiful, nor pacific in our experience. Despite Dramamine and Hyoscine, I was sick most of the voyage. Even Bill became a little bored with the great quantities of reading he did when it was too cold, windy and damp to play deck games.

We sailed into Sydney Harbour at daylight on October 12, 1952 after completing a 12,000 mile journey. On this day, like Columbus, we discovered a new land, indeed a new continent. This was the land of the marsupial, of the gum tree and exotic bird life, of sheep and cattle, of antiquated railways and modern airplanes, a desert and nullarbour and an unique university.

That Christmas, in a letter to friends, I described Canberra as "an artificial city, growing out of jealousy between New South Wales and Victoria, planned to be a city for government. It has a population of 25,000, and is situated in the Southern Tableland, surrounded by low hills of ever changing beauty. The silver birches, hay trees, wattle, plum and pin oak vie with the ubiquitous native gum or eucalyptus for the admiring glances of the stroller. The roses, lilies, pansies and sweet peas are blooming.

"The city is spread out to a ridiculous extent, indicating that great growth is expected, but we wonder if it will ever be achieved. There are three shopping centres, with rather inferior merchandise, two cinemas which feature mostly second-rate American movies, and the occasional good picture from Hollywood, England or France.

"We like the Australian gadget called an electric jug, an earthenware jug with an electric unit inside to heat water in two minutes. We like the social custom of morning and afternoon tea. However, the inconvenience of everyday living and the cold of the climate are overcome by the warmth of the people and their many kindnesses to us…"

"Shopping is most confusing, with wieners sold in a furniture store, roses sold in a butcher shop, poor selection of fresh food, and most inferior clothes and furniture. There is one book store, of exceptionally high quality, run by the wife of a professor."

Daily living was rudimentary and the summer heat made it even more challenging. Thinking back though, it was a wonderful experience. We lived in a six-room furnished house in the outer suburbs of Canberra where we learned to cope with the difficulties of domestic life. We grew our fruit and vegetables by necessity. I learned to cook on a woodstove and boil my clothes in a copper boiler. Bill learned how to chop wood. You didn't just turn on the tap to have a bath. It was an event that began with heating your water in a wood-chip heater. You had to plan to stay home on a particular night to wash your hair and bathe! Shopping was difficult in this city because it had no main street.

My first foray into the culinary world of preserving produced some quite edible results.

During the year, we got to know Australia and Australians and found both to be intriguing to us. We visited Sydney and Brisbane, stayed at a sheep station and toured a number of smaller centres in New South Wales. The appearance of the land was very different from that of North America. Australia was a colourless land pervaded with the grey-green dustiness of the eucalyptus. The only brilliance to be found was in the sky and the gaily-coloured plumage of the rosellas, gelahs, parrots, magpies, cockatoos, and kookaburras. Country towns reflected the same drabness with their unpainted buildings, galvanized iron roofs and fences, and the ever-present wooden awnings.

In contrast with the loneliness of the countryside was the friendliness of the people. Everywhere we went, whether in Canberra, Sydney, Cootamundra, Temora, Armidale or Tamworth, we were made welcome and royally entertained. Australians were the most active party-goers in the world. No incident was too trivial to provide a reason for a party.

We were there during a time when Australian themes were increasingly being used in literature, arts and music. Australian history and politics were in vogue and there was a movement to make Canberra the political and cultural capital. The creation of Australian graduate training in place of overseas training was part of that plan. Its success would depend on overcoming a type of prejudice that existed in the minds of educated Australians who coveted the chance to study at an English or North American University.

The Australian National University was planned in 1946, and the first faculty member arrived in 1949. The buildings were still temporary and there was much construction of housing, laboratories and libraries. We were part of a pioneer enterprise and it was both exciting and frustrating. Initially, we had stayed in a university hostel—a boarding house cum hotel—until we found suitable housing. Ross Hohnen, the registrar, and his wife Phyllis became our good friends.

The university was devoted exclusively to postgraduate research. A bachelor's degree was the prerequisite for admission. Bill had a distinguished academic record having attained three degrees and a research fellowship. He had graduated with first class honours and as gold medalist of his class with a Bachelor of Arts in history from the University of Toronto in 1940. Bill earned his Masters and Ph.D. from Brown University in Providence, Rhode Island. Bill was elected as a graduate member of Phi Beta Kappa in acknowledgement of the high academic standards he had achieved while he pursued his Ph.D. Rarely had this honour been extended to a Ph.D.

This was an exhilarating time which held all kinds of new experiences—from adjusting to the new monetary system of pounds, and shillings and pence to talking *Strine* and mastering the Australian accent. Bill didn't go there to lecture but he was asked to teach Australian politics to diplomatic cadets.

Bill found his work most stimulating and spent long hours at his desk and in the library. He also joined the university cricket team. Initially, I spent my time reading and assisting with a survey of immigration in the university's Department of Demography.

I continued to be the most educated B.A.-less woman in the world, this time during a school year which ran from March through November. The University of Melbourne's Canberra University College refused to give me credit for courses taken at American universities, so I started over again. I studied British economic history, Australian political history, psychology and Australian literature.

In January, I was offered a job I could not possibly turn down. I replaced the executive director of the Australian Vice-Chancellors' Committee who was taking a sabbatical for one year. It turned out to be a two-year term in which we lobbied for government funding and support on behalf of 10 Australian universities, and worked on more than 3,000 scholarships for overseas students. This committee's equivalent is the Association of Universities and Colleges of Canada, a council of university presidents.

Bill and I were quite keen on the Canberra Repertory Theatre and worked on several productions. I took part in *"Government Inspector"* by Chekhov and *"His Excellency."* We played the American Colonel and his wife in *"Love of Four Colonels"* and Bill played a dinosaur and I was a good time girl in *"Skin of Our Teeth."*

Australia had been our home for just over a year when tragedy struck. We had no way of knowing what was to be. In a Christmas letter to our friends, we wished them as good a year in 1954 as we had in 1953. Just before Christmas of 1953, Bill's duodenal ulcer haemorrhaged. An operation was scheduled immediately. I don't believe an operation would have been a serious consideration in Canada or the United States but that is what they did in Australia. Who was I to question this? I was not a doctor.

Bill had been hospitalized previously with ulcers and was treated successfully with blood transfusions. The medical advice of the day was to control Bill's diet carefully with mild foods—which is why I never really learned how to cook properly—and to limit stress for the rest of his life. How do you keep a man of 32 or 33 from having any stress? You just can't. All sorts of things happened. Bill lost jobs. He worried about many things. That is one of the reasons we didn't have children. I did not want to add to that stress, and I did not want to risk the chance of having to raise children without a husband the way Mother did.

Bill had the best of surgeons and tremendous support. People, such as Ross Hohnen and Bill's faculty colleagues and fellow university cricket players, rallied around him by donating blood for his transfusions. The hospital did not have a blood bank and blood was not tested.

I remember standing outside on the hospital veranda when Ross jokingly said, "Your husband is a veritable United Nations" because of the multi-national composition of the donors. I laughed at the time and responded, in jest, by posing a series of questions I had to answer as a potential blood donor when Bill needed transfusions in the United States. As a donor, I was asked whether I was pregnant, had had any major surgeries or had ever been affected by malaria or any social diseases. It was too late when I learned that one of Bill's Australian donors had contracted malaria, reportedly a common occurrence among Australian soldiers.

The operation on Bill's ulcer was successful which made his sudden death even more tragic and unexpected. Bill had been infected by a blood transfusion. I had arrived at the hospital early Sunday morning to discover his temperature was 105 degrees. My husband died three days before Christmas. It was a dreadful time. I hadn't expected to lose Bill to death. He had this same trouble before but he always came through. He wasn't well but he did a tremendous amount with his life. He was very active. He played sports and he taught and he loved young people. I was engulfed by that familiar and desperate feeling of loneliness, once again. It would stay with me for a very long time after.

Canada's High Commissioner Arthur Irwin who was a former editor of *Maclean's* Magazine, and his wife P.K. Page, now a famous Canadian poet, came to the hospital to take me to their home. I was agonizing over how to tell Bill's parents, but Arthur volunteered to telephone them for me. You can imagine getting that message so close to Christmas and being so very far away. Bill's parents knew Bill was sick because I had told them, but this news came without warning.

On December 24, a Requiem Eucharist Service was held at our church, the Church of St. John the Baptist. Bill's mother wanted him sent home but transporting a body 10,000 miles was terribly complicated and very expensive. I was advised to have him cremated. To make matters worse, I came down with pleurisy. Some of our friends, including my boss, John Ford, took his body to Sydney for cremation and a brief ceremony before Bill's ashes were returned to his family in Canada. Our friends urged me not to attempt the trip to Sydney. A service at St. Clement's Church in Toronto was followed by interment at Markham, Ontario where the Rolph family originated.

Bill was mourned by friends and colleagues on two continents.

> *"I am greatly grieved to hear of the passing of Dr.*
> *Rolph. His initiative and enterprise were well known to me and*
> *I had anticipated long and interesting discussions on those topics*
> *in which we were mutually interested when he completed his first*
> *phase of research. His extraordinary knowledge of Australian*
> *rural affairs and his deep insight into the problems of the*
> *countryside in Canada and in Australia made him a particularly*

welcome visitor. My colleagues and I will never cease to regret
that he has not been spared to complete a task of inestimable
value to Australia and to which he devoted himself with such
marked ability and diligence. His loss is irreparable. My deepest
sympathy goes to Mrs. Rolph and members of his family."

Sir Arthur Fadden, Commonwealth Treasurer
and leader of the Australian Country Party

"I have lost not only a personal friend whose lovable
characteristics endeared him to all who had the good fortune to
know him; he was also an extremely able guide and tutor in a
particular field of my own political activities. As author of the
history of the Australian Country Party, now in the course of
publication, I found in Dr. Rolph a critic whose profound
knowledge of the subject marked him as a brilliant political
philosopher and a wise counselor."

Ulrich Ellis

"The death of an able scholar must always come as a
grave and almost personal loss to a small academic community
like Canada, but the shock seems greater when the loss is that of
a promising young man passing not with the list of titles and
honours which mark a lifetime of achievement but with the
hope of what might have been. Yet in his brief time, William
Rolph compressed a full life of energy and accomplishment.

"He received a major research fellowship at the
National University of Australia to study the history of the
Australian Country Party. This in large measure was recog-
nition of the scholarship he had displayed in studying aspects of
Canadian farmers' movements and his valuable biography
Henry Wise Wood of Alberta. He died with his work unfinished
but its quality and his own received ample testimony and warm
tributes paid him by leading Australian scholars and public
men. Kindly, eager, effervescent, William Rolph had a gift for
laughter and friendship. He was the rare, sweet nature that
leaves many to mourn him."

J.M.S. Careless, Canadian Historical Review

I accepted Georges and Jacqueline Charpentier's invitation to stay with them until I left Australia six months later. Our friends were supportive and compassionate. The executive director wanted me to stay on the job, and university faculty encouraged me to continue my undergraduate studies by offering me accommodation at a new residence.

Among the university friends who invited me to dinner were Charlie Price and Alison Cheek. They were married and had small children. I was moaning and groaning about Bill's death and the fact that I had no money when Charlie said to me: "Ruth, we feel very sorry for you. It is a terrible thing that you have lost Bill because he was a wonderful man. But frankly, if you don't stop being so self-centred, you are not going to have any friends. You get busy and get out there and do other things. We are not interested in your problems."

At the time, I thought they were cruel. But it was the kindest thing anyone could have said to me. I would try to overcome my terrible feelings of loneliness by doing things for and with others.

Coming home alone

Bill was an only child and his parents were very upset. They were very fond of me and wanted me to come home. I really couldn't decide to live in Australia for the rest of my life. There were just too many decisions to make all at once. I started my journey back to Canada by freighter in July of 1954.

I am on the last leg of my return trip home sailing along the St. Lawrence River en route to Montreal in August 1954.

Before I left, I gave away our two cats that Bill had named Coca and Cola to some good Australian friends, John and Vona Dean. I was told later Coca and Cola had kittens. They kept one and called it Pepsi.

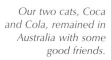

Our two cats, Coca and Cola, remained in Australia with some good friends.

I traveled across Australia to join seven other passengers boarding a freighter at Bunbury, 100 miles south of Perth. I was to sail to Cape Town, South Africa, Dakar, Senegal, the Canary Islands, and disembark at Liverpool before going on to Canada. I didn't have very much money. In fact, I had 18 Australian shillings in my pocket and I was very concerned because I had no way of providing gratuities to the staff on the freighter. I just didn't know what I was going to do.

Occasionally after dinner, the passengers played cards with the officers. One evening, poker, a game I didn't know how to play, was suggested. Once they showed me how, I told them I couldn't afford to play because I had no money. I don't remember how we got around that obstacle. Suffice is to say, I made enough money playing poker to provide tips to the staff and to pay for my train ticket from Liverpool to London where I visited some Australian friends, Fred Ordish and his wife Peggy. I haven't played poker since. I took a trip to Paris and Scandinavia before boarding a freighter in August at Hull, England. The *Prinses*

Irene sailed to Rotterdam before we began the voyage across the Atlantic Ocean to Québec City and Montreal. Along the way, I formed lifetime friendships with a New York couple and an English gentleman who lives in Toronto.

Bill's mother, Maidie, and one of Bill's friends, Don Eldon, were kind enough to meet me in Montreal. Bill's friends at the University of Toronto made arrangements to admit me as an undergraduate and secured a job for me as a don at St. Hilda's College. That entitled me to free room and board.

Maidie and Frank opened their home to me and encouraged me to finish university. I stayed with them whenever I wasn't in residence and until I obtained employment in Ottawa.

A degree at last!
Five universities, three countries, two continents & 10 years later

Mother was not too pleased with me spending my time at university because widows worked! I graduated from the University of Toronto with a Bachelor of Arts (B.A.) in Political Economy in 1955. I was one of three women in the graduating class. Mother refused to attend the graduation but she did give me a bible to commemorate the event. Bill's mother and father attended, as did Ross and Phyllis Hohnen who had interrupted their world tour to be there.

Maidie and Frank Rolph encouraged me to pursue my degree. Maidie Rolph, left, and Phyllis Hohnen, right, and her husband, Ross, attended my graduation ceremonies at the University of Toronto. (Kurshan & Lang Colour Service)

Receiving my B.A. was an extraordinary feeling. I thought I was on the top of the world. I had really achieved something. The B.A. was one of the major achievements of my life. I had worked so hard. I had studied at five universities in three countries, on two continents over a decade. I went forward two steps and fell back one, and I did a lot of work. Tulane didn't like the courses I had taken, and Australia had no regard for American education, so each time, I had to start over again. The only times I went to university full-time were in Tulane and in my last year at Toronto. When I finally got to Toronto, I had to take four fourth year honours courses including political science and economics, one fourth year course in literature, one third year course in religious knowledge and a second year course in geography. I worked hard earning my keep as a don. I was very pleased and very proud of myself.

Next on my list was a visit to my high school to see the principal who had insisted I was not university material. With my degree in hand, I went to St. Clement's School and said to her, "Look at this!" Some 35 years later, I was the recipient of St. Clement's Gold Award—awarded every five years "to alumnae whose achievements embody the qualities and values St.Clement's instils in its students— integrity, resourcefulness, responsibility

When I received my Bachelor of Arts in Political Economy, I felt I was on top of the world!

and trustworthiness." I was chosen by a selection committee consisting of alumnae and was presented with a watch and $500. The money was reinvested in an award recognizing senior students who perform community volunteer work.

My university professors urged me to do postgraduate work. One, in particular, suggested law school even though few women studied law. The law and specifically constitutional matters were of great interest to me. I took the time to talk to lawyers to learn what it would take to become a lawyer, only to conclude that it would be too difficult for me because I was a young widow with no money, and I didn't have the wherewithal to do battle. In fact, I was offered two fellowships— one from Upsala University in Sweden and the second from the University of Toronto to pursue graduate work in economic history and political science. I didn't speak Swedish so that ruled out Upsala. Financially, I didn't have enough money to cover living expenses while I did postgraduate work at Toronto which is why I applied for a scholarship from the University Women's Club (UWC) in Toronto. My application was declined on the basis that if a woman hadn't proven herself by the age of 30, she wasn't going to achieve anything. I happened to be a very elderly 34. I got mad, and as soon as I was in a position to influence a change in that policy to recognize older women, I did. I joined the UWC in Ottawa in September of 1955, soon after I started my first job.

What's a million?
The Conservative sweep and how politics doesn't behave the way you think it should

The theories I had learned as a student of political science and economics were about to be tested by the realities of politics when I was hired as a researcher by the Progressive Conservative (PC) Party of Canada in Ottawa. The PCs were rebuilding and members were eager to return to power after 20 years in opposition. The potency of power and impassionate personalities would create some dramatic dynamics.

> *"Bill died. Ruth came back to Montreal and Bill's mother Maidie and I met her there. Ruth was quite sad about Bill's death. She wanted to get into politics in some way. She now had to make her own way financially. As Director of Research for the Progressive Conservative Party, I knew the new research department was expanding.*
>
> *"As it happened, this was a timely comment that Ruth made because it seemed to me, she would fit very well into the expansion of our research. I had a very good idea of how this would work. We had done some studies and I had a good relationship with the Caucus Research Committee, chaired by Donald M. Flemming. The other members were Rolly Michener who later became the Governor General and J.M. MacDonnell. The idea was to do some serious political research, not just write speeches for members of Parliament. All the work we did was funnelled through that committee. If you let the members loose on the research department individually, they would want you to do their speeches and pamphlets.*
>
> *"I needed a research assistant so I asked Ruth to consider coming to Ottawa. It was necessary to consult the*

*National Director on the hiring. The national Director was Bill
Rowe, the son of Earl Rowe, MP for Dufferin-Simcoe. Earl
had been a senior member of the PC Party for a long time, and
briefly served as a Minister in R.B. Bennett's PC Government
(1930-1935). Both Earl Rowe and Bill Rowe loved harness
racing. I knew Ruth well enough that she would be able to do
this job with its political angle. It was tailor-made as a first
approach to politics. Ruth came to Headquarters, an old yellow
brick house at 141 Laurier Avenue West which had been
purchased for the PC Party by Dick Bell, a PC national
director. (In fact, Ruth recalls that Dick, who became Ruth's
second husband, used his own money to purchase the property
for $7,000 and a decade later, it sold for $150,000—making
a tidy profit for the PC Party.)*

*"I introduced Ruth to Bill Rowe. His immediate
response was, 'We are leaving for Montreal and I have a
taxi waiting. Come with us. We have a race this afternoon
at Blue Bonnett.'*

*"It was the strangest interview, I am sure, Ruth ever
had. I don't think much was said about politics or research or
anything maybe but horses. I don't know whether Bill won or
lost that day, but Ruth got the job. We hired another person, Bill
Morrow. The research department was doing fine under George
Drew. There were successes in Parliament. Morale was high."*

Don Eldon

The pace was frenetic but exhilarating. As an economic researcher working with
Don Eldon, I analyzed election issues and results, researched speeches for MPs,
edited *The Progress Report*, scrutinized papers for policy guidance, and
produced and distributed party literature. I worked on four by-elections, one
provincial campaign, one leadership convention, and the 1957 general election.

The PC Party headquarters staff was a very small group, unlike the huge Parliamentarian staffs or the large offices of today. Our small and intimate research team consisted of Don, Ruth Loomer, Ann Baird, Bill Morrow, and me. Typically, staff support for an MP consisted of a secretary. Today, each MP has staff and access to Parliamentary Library researchers. I am not passing judgment. Whether or not larger staffs are a good thing is a matter for debate.

The other part of our team was led by Dalton Camp, our Director of Public Relations and the first experienced advertising agency man to work for the PC Party. Dalton was valued for his knowledge of Maritime politics, and he was widely credited with Manitoba Premier Duff Roblin's ascension to power.

I couldn't help noticing the painted wires running throughout our Laurier offices which prompted my question to Don.

Don was quick to reply. "You know what this was? This was a house of ill-repute. Those painted wires were telephone lines and they were connected to every room. Clients were telephoned and warned when a police raid was imminent!"

Flora MacDonald was my secretary at the time. She had come up from Nova Scotia in search of employment. In 1972, Flora was elected as MP for the constituency of Kingston and the Islands. The Hon. Flora MacDonald went on to hold three Cabinet posts between 1979 and 1988.

One of my first assignments in 1955 was to work with MP Ellen Louks Fairclough to draft "equal pay for equal work" legislation. The only way Ellen could introduce the bill was as a private member's bill because she was a member of the Opposition. Private members' bills seldom received the support of the party in power. Nevertheless, one year later, legislation entrenching equal pay for equal work within the Federal Government was passed.

Ellen had a successful track record of pursing women's issues. Earlier in the 1950s, Ellen pressed for the creation of a Women's Bureau within the Department of Labour. It became a reality in 1954. In fact, Freda Paltiel, a good friend of mine, was the director of the Women's Bureau for many years. Her husband, Khayyam Paltiel, was my thesis advisor at Carleton University, years later.

Our research team dealt with issues of the day such as determining the Party's position on the General Agreement on Tariffs and Trade and examining the Social Credit Party which had its roots in Alberta. It was important to distinguish our Party from Social Credit because in the public's mind, there wasn't much difference. My knowledge of my husband's thesis on agrarian politics helped immensely in that research. Don did the economic assessment and I did the philosophical assessment.

When the 1956 provincial election was called in Nova Scotia, Dalton Camp went down to run the campaign. He sent for me and my typewriter. I spent several weeks at the Lord Nelson Hotel, writing speeches and helping to organize the campaign and the advertising. North American consumer demand for television was on the rise. I remember coaching Bob Stanfield who was about to appear in his first television interview. Bob Stanfield's Conservatives won that election. He served as Premier from 1956 to 1967 until he became the federal PC Party Leader, a position he held from 1967 to 1977.

Under the Hon. George Drew's leadership, the federal Progressive Conservatives managed to embarrass the ruling Liberal Government on the defence production debate. That debate merely set the stage for the next very major debacle: the Trans-Canada pipeline debate in the House of Commons in 1956. The Liberals, led by the Rt. Hon. Louis St. Laurent, were planning to pass legislation to expropriate land to build a natural gas pipeline from Alberta to Ontario and Québec.

The Conservatives worked hard to keep the focus on the raucous debate. Voters didn't forget the Liberal Minister of Trade and Commerce the Hon. C.D. Howe's infamous remark, "What's a million (dollars)?" as he defended the skyrocketing costs of the pipeline. The expulsion of the Hon. Don Fleming from the House of Commons for his remarks during one of the exchanges presented Ellen Fairclough with the opportunity to drape a Canadian flag over Don's vacant seat in the House. But just as public sentiment in support of George Drew and the Progressive Conservative Party was building, George Drew tendered his resignation for health reasons. The search was on for a new leader and the national leadership convention was called for December of 1956.

Dick Bell and Léon Balcer were joint co-chairs of the first ever, televised Canadian political leadership convention. My job was to issue accreditation to the news media and to provide logistical support such as expediting television equipment requirements, and to some extent with Dalton's guidance, arranging media interviews.

A leadership convention was a very good device to publicize a political party and its policies. Traditionally at conventions, the Liberals or the Conservatives, as the case may be, debated policy issues and decided which issues would form the planks in the platform. Delegates came prepared to express the views of their particular ridings in a public forum, the proceedings of which were reported by the news media. Almost a decade later, I would explore the use of the convention to select the party leader and the role of the news media in my thesis leading to a Master's degree in political science.

John George Diefenbaker, who had lost to George Drew in the 1942 and 1948 leadership conventions, won the 1956 leadership on the first ballot against Donald Flemming and E. Davey Fulton.

The Liberals' move to invoke closure to end the Trans-Canada pipeline debate vexed the now attentive voters who responded by electing a PC minority government in 1957. It was almost a surprise. Voters sent a stronger message when the 1958 general federal election produced a Conservative sweep. Not only were more PC MPs elected than ever before including Dick Bell, the 1958 election produced the largest majority in the history of Canadian Parliament. That was also the year the Lester (Mike) Pearson became leader of the Liberal Party.

Donald Fleming, a leadership contender in the 1948 and 1956 conventions, was appointed Minister of Finance by the Right Hon. John Diefenbaker. J.M. MacDonnell was appointed Minister without Portfolio, Roland Michener Speaker of the House, Dick Bell Parliamentary Secretary to the Minister of Finance and Ellen Fairclough became the first woman ever to be appointed to a Cabinet post when she was named Secretary of State. In 1958, Ellen became Minister of Citizenship and Immigration and in 1963 Post-Master General. During her 13-year elected tenure, she was the only woman in the history of Canadian Parliament to serve as acting Prime Minister. Her Majesty Queen Elizabeth II bestowed the title "The Right Honourable" on Ellen in 1992.

Following his 1957 election as the 13th Prime Minister of Canada and the first Conservative Prime Minister in 22 years, John Diefenbaker dismissed most of the PC Headquarters staff including me. From my perspective, Diefenbaker was a very strange man and very difficult to work with. Diefenbaker didn't want to have his authority questioned in any way. It may be that he believed people who were loyal to George Drew could not be loyal to him. From my lowly position, Diefenbaker was not as considerate of staff as George Drew was. On the other hand, a friend of mine absolutely adored Diefenbaker. By that time, I had learned that politics was a pretty tough game. It doesn't always behave the way you think it ought to behave. The Trans-Canada pipeline—the world's largest natural gas pipeline at the time—was completed in 1958 at a cost of $375 million.

CHAPTER THREE

A Woman's Place is *Where?*

Out of the kitchen and into the fray

Mrs. R. A. Bell calls on women to light a light for education

Mrs. Ruth M. Bell Believes Politics Is Everybody's Business

Employment in the public service was out of the question because I was an American citizen so I accepted an invitation from a friend to come to Montreal.

I loved living in Montreal. It was a wonderful place with many art galleries to visit and concerts to enjoy. There was plenty of walking to do. Québec City's winter carnival hosted by Bonhomme, a lovable snowman, was quite enjoyable. I had an apartment in Notre Dame de Gras for several years. Later, I shared an interesting, old apartment in Westmount with Marguerite Cheyne who became a lifetime friend. I attended her 90th birthday.

While in Montreal, I renewed my membership in the English Speaking Union which had been formed in England before the Second World War to establish a dialogue among English-speaking countries. It was purely a cultural effort, not a political effort. A friend of mine had introduced me to the Ottawa chapter headed by Mrs. Ethel Pearly-Robertson when I worked with the Progressive

Conservatives. I have been a member ever since. In fact, the Ottawa chapter marked its 50th anniversary in October 2003 with guest speaker Russell Mills, the former publisher of the Ottawa Citizen.

I was hired as secretary to the president of Clark Foods, a small family business. It was a job that didn't last long. Here's what happened. Customarily, the president took his senior officers to a retreat for a day or two in the Laurentians. Naturally, as secretary, I made the arrangements and was required to attend. Once the meetings concluded, we had dinner. A couple of the senior officials asked me to dance. I didn't think much of it until the next day when I was fired by a very angry president who said I should have known my place as a secretary.

Being fired for that reason came as a surprise to me and to several of his senior officers who knew I was a very capable employee. Give Mr. Clark credit though. He did give me several weeks to find another job.

Soon after, I was hired as a research economist at the Bank of Montreal's Head Office in Montreal—a position I held from 1957 to 1962.

The Bank of Montreal valued my advice on financial contributions to political parties and frequently sent me to represent the Bank in consultations with other financial advisors in Ottawa. When federal budgets came down in Ottawa, I was the bank's representative in the briefing lock-up.

Dominion-provincial financial relationships, which were defined by frequent arguments on jurisdiction and authority, were another hot topic. It was a question of how to get along with one another. Today, that challenge persists.

Contemporary issues were addressed in a series of articles I authored in the Bank of Montreal's *Business Review*. They included: *Fiscal Federalism* (1960), *Electing a President* (1960), *Canada's Expanding Universities* (1961), *Manpower and Employment* (1961) and *Electing a Canadian Government* (1962). The articles on American and Canadian elections were reprinted until the early 1970s to meet the demand from American schools and universities.

One of my goals as an economic researcher was to try to persuade the Federal Government's Dominion Statistics to add new census questions to more accurately portray the impact of economic sectors including the volunteer sector on the Gross National Product (GNP). I believed the value of work performed by volunteers needed to be measured and the value recognized as a contributor to the GNP and to society. It took 25 years to recognize the role of the volunteer, but those questions were added finally. I will tell you more about that later in this story.

We also had an informal network of bank economists who shared information at dinner meetings hosted by our respective banks. It was in this milieu that I met several bank presidents, including Earle McLaughlin with whom I was destined to have an acrimonious, lengthy exchange that produced positive results, years later.

Chief Economist Ted Walton and his wife had us to dinner at their home. Looking back, we were a small group that got along well, but there were times when things were less than ideal.

The concrete ceiling:
Women don't have families to support!

It was at the Bank of Montreal where I experienced another face of discrimination. As part of my compensation, I inquired about the pension plan. At the time, there were no women bank officers or managers. Male bank employees contributed six per cent annually to a retirement plan and were eligible for group life insurance equivalent to two years' salary. Women employees, who retired at 65, were entitled to a retirement allowance on good behaviour in amounts determined solely by the employer, with no contribution from the employee and no group insurance because "women had no dependents." I pressed the pension plan issue.

"No," I was told emphatically. "That can't be done because you are a woman and women don't have families to support."

"Well, I do have to contribute to my mother's support and I want to look after my own old age," I replied.

"No, you are only eligible for the retirement allowance on good behaviour," was the response.

When I asked for a salary higher than the bank was paying female economists, officials initially were stunned, but eventually paid it noting that all other salaries in the economics department would have to be increased.

There was one more perk to which I was entitled: a safety deposit box, conditional on my husband's approval or so I was told. The prevailing law in Québec assumed that when a woman married, her husband would support her forever.

"Oh, are you going to pay my way up to heaven so I can get my husband's permission?" I asked the officer.

He was floored. "You aren't married?" he asked.

"No, I am a widow," I said.

"Do you have a son?" he asked.

"No, I don't have a son," I replied. I learned later that a friend in a similar position had her 10-year-old son sign the document. That incident started me worrying. I couldn't do much about it because I wasn't going to jeopardize my job by kicking up a fuss. But in the course of my work, I consulted with the bank president, Mr. Hart, on the newsletters. He was a nice guy. I told him I didn't think women were treated fairly at the bank. He acknowledged that fact but said there wasn't much he could do about it.

Over the years, similar incidents occurred. I was being reminded constantly of women's subordinate status and I had yet to decide what to do about it. The attitude towards women was very annoying given what I knew about women, like Mother, who successfully supported their families. We didn't have as much talk about single mothers then and I don't think marriage broke up as regularly as it does today. There were probably some unhappy marriages, but husbands and wives didn't do much about it.

I was working in Montreal when Mother died early in January, 1960. She had suffered from high blood pressure for years. The doctor had warned me when I was a teenager that Mother might be ill-tempered from time to time, as a result.

I received a call on a Sunday morning, just after the holiday season. Mother had suffered either a stroke or a heart attack and was in the hospital. When I phoned my boss, he brought me enough money to buy an airline ticket to Toronto. In those days, there were no credit cards—at least I didn't have one—and banks were closed on Sundays.

Bill's mother, Maidie, opened up her home to me, and my good friend, Doris, drove me to the hospital. Mother was unconscious so she wasn't aware I was with her on Sunday or on Monday. Her death early Tuesday morning was a blessing. Father was buried in Atlanta but Mother was buried with her mother in a mausoleum in St. Thomas, according to her wishes. Mother left me her household goods including the hen with the red wax eyes.

I am not objective enough to analyse the relationship Mother and I had, except to say, it was rather complex, but I certainly admired her for what she did for me. She did it at a time when it was very, very difficult for women. She went into a field where it was almost impossible for women to succeed but she did. She wasn't a member of high society, but she did her job above and beyond reproach. Even now, I look back and admire her for what she accomplished.

Marriage was in the air when I was in Montreal. One of my Australian friends, Pierre who was posted to New York, would come up to see me in Montreal every once in a while. We were seriously considering marriage, but first, I would have to become a Roman Catholic because he wasn't prepared to leave the Church. I didn't believe there was a great difference between a Roman Catholic and an Anglican so I began taking instructions from a priest at Montreal's Loyola College. Before we started, the priest said: "In all honesty, I have more difficulty converting Anglicans than any other religious group. There is just something about it. I think Anglicans and Roman Catholics are too similar, but I am willing to try if you are!" he said.

I took the lessons. They were very, very interesting; however, I could not accept the concept that the Pope was infallible. Pierre and I did not marry.

A new chapter: Teaching politics

My formal education continued when I enrolled to study public finance as a part-time student at Sir George Williams University (now Concordia) in Montreal. I had planned to work on my Masters at McGill University on a part-time basis but McGill only offered courses on a full-time basis and I needed to work. As a bank employee, I attended *"Learned Societies"* meetings usually held in May or June. Various segments of the liberal arts belonged to the Learned Societies and it was an excellent way to keep in touch with people in my field. My group consisted of political scientists, economists, psychologists, sociologists, historians and anthropologists.

Little did I know that a Learned Societies' members' meeting at the Université de Montreal would set the next chapter of my life in motion. I knew quite a few members. Maurice Careless, who was head of the University of Toronto's History Department and my late husband Bill's best man at our wedding, was among the historians in attendance as was Ken McKirdy. Ken and his wife Margaret, and Bill and I were good friends in Australia. Paul Cornell, another historian who went to university with Bill, was there too. Paul was to become an important part of my later life.

As Chair of the new University of Waterloo's History Department, Paul was recruiting staff for teaching positions in economics and political science. Ken was one of his recent appointees. I didn't think much about it at first, until Paul and Ken invited me to an interview at Waterloo. I stayed with Ken and Margaret.

It was a busy day. Without any warning, I was asked to give two lectures—one to Paul's morning class about the impending election and the second to Ken's afternoon class. In between, I met the Bishop and the Dean for an interview over lunch. They were conducting a search for the Dean of Renison College. Renison College was an Anglican residential college named in memory of Archbishop Robert John Renison (1875-1957). Founded in 1959, the college was moved to the campus of the University of Waterloo in 1962. As we began our lunch, I discovered I was the only one there who actually had known Archbishop Renison.

According to his biography *One Day at a Time*, Robert John Renison traveled down the Albany River to James Bay in 1898. He was said to be the first white man to make the 750-mile journey by canoe. He was elected Bishop of Athabasca in 1932, but within the first year, he was persuaded to take the rectorship of St. Paul's Anglican Church in Toronto where he served for 11 years. I was confirmed by him. One of his sons, George, was in my circle of friends. George and I went out a few times together. When I told the Rector I knew his son, he scolded me and told me I should go out with better people. He was just teasing. Time passed. When the war broke out, George enlisted and had an illustrious war career. I haven't seen George since. Robert John Renison was elected as Bishop by the Diocese of Moosonee in 1943 where he worked until his retirement in 1954. The bishops of the Church honoured Bishop Renison by electing him the Metropolitan Archbishop of Ontario in 1952.

Unbeknownst to me, Ken McKirdy had sent a memorandum to Paul Cornell, dated January 8, 1962, to outline my educational and professional background, and the pros and cons of hiring me. I have often said you don't see yourself as others see you. Ken wrote in part:

"…She is an officer, no other material. She would not be willing to serve as the department's Girl Friday. She has ideas of her own which she would expect to be given consideration… She is an extremely intelligent person. I know of more than one Ph.D. who breathed easier when she decided not to take his class… Her analysis of constituency voting patterns is possibly the most thorough ever done in Canada. Professor John Meisel of Queens has praised them and the author…

"…She has editorial experience as Editor of the PC House Journal and now is one of the editors of the Bank of Montreal's Business Review. I append a copy of one of her recent pieces: Canada's Expanding Universities. She was a don in residence at St. Hilda's College in Toronto. She might be suitable as dean…

"…I confess a personal bias in her favour though I wonder how the faculty wives' association would react to an appointment of an extremely attractive widow who does not look the 40 years my arithmetic tells me she must have lived…."

Ken McKirdy

I was appointed as the new Dean of Renison College and as a political science instructor. I would teach a graduate course in contemporary political ideology and two undergraduate courses. I liked being with young people and enjoyed teaching.

Just as I was leaving to teach at Waterloo, Bill's father died. I flew to Toronto and went straight to the funeral parlour. One of my gentlemen friends came to fetch me and my 18-pound tabby cat, Sandy, after the funeral to drive us to Waterloo. He likes to tell the story about how Sandy peed on his brand new coat in the back seat of his car. Sandy was much loved by my students. Sandy got the casting call when some of these students who were doing a reading on CBC Radio required a cat to say "meow, meow."

On one occasion, I was entertaining the Bishop and two or three of the clergy in my tiny apartment at Waterloo. We were sipping sherry before going to dinner in the residential dining room. Sandy loved parties and particularly getting up on laps. The Bishop wanted to know his name. "I named him Sandy because of his sandy-beige coloured tummy," I explained.

The Bishop protested, "You can't call a distinguished fellow like that…Sandy. He has such a military bearing. We must have a more distinguished name." So they came up with Sandhurst, the name of a military college in England.

Sandhurst, my 18-pound tabby cat, moved with me to Waterloo. He lived with me for 21 years.

Politics: Go in with your vacuum cleaner and clean it up!

As Dean and lecturer, I was asked to address local community groups. Public speaking engagements provided a venue to solicit women's reactions to proposed university lectures on a variety of topics as well as the status of women. Waterloo was one of the leaders in anticipating the needs of women with children by providing daycare services as part of its course offerings. It also was distinguished by its work-study program in which students alternated between studies and practical work place experience.

These speaking engagements provided me with the platform to urge women to become more involved in building their community by participating in local politics and to advance from there. The *Kitchener-Waterloo Record's* coverage of my speech to the local branch of the National Secretaries Association on Thursday, October 4, 1962 highlighted women's participation in politics as players. "Women definitely have a place in politics but not necessarily confined to women's organizations. Women should be absorbed in the overall political organization. She should be considered as a human being, not a woman."

I was convinced many people were looking for something in which to believe, beyond their religious beliefs and I was of the opinion that joining a political party could meet that need. It was a message I delivered throughout the 1960s and 1970s. Politics is everybody's business. Don't forget, people who criticize party leaders or their politics are really criticizing themselves because it is they who elected them. Women used to tell me that they weren't interested in running for political office because politics was dirty. My reply was: "You are a housekeeper. If politics is dirty, go in with your vacuum cleaner and clean it up."

Educating engineering students

Waterloo's Faculty of Engineering was new. The powers that be decided engineering students would be required to take some social sciences in addition to engineering courses. As a political science lecturer, I was appointed as the professorial link between the Faculty of Social Sciences and the Faculty of Engineering. That meant I needed to attend the latter's meetings. My first one was memorable. I marched over to the School of Engineering to look for the faculty meeting room. In due course, I knew I was at the right location because when I opened the door I recognized a few of the many men who sat around the table. There were no women faculty members and few women took engineering courses.

The Dean of Engineering looked my way and said, "Young woman, this is the School of Engineering's faculty meeting."

"Yes sir," I replied.

"Well, would you please leave the room? You are not invited."

"I have been appointed as a representative of the Faculty of Liberal Arts to the Faculty of Engineering and I will be teaching political science to your engineering students!" I retorted.

He was dumbfounded. He looked askance at me, but luckily a few of the men, who recognized me, asked me to sit down beside them. At that moment, the Dean was very unhappy with me.

The engineering students had never been taught by a woman lecturer before and they didn't like what I was teaching. I reminded them that they didn't have to attend my classes but they did have to pass the examination in order to obtain a credit. Otherwise, they were wasting their money.

When I entered the lecture hall for the first time, the young fellows were lounging around in chairs. On the teacher's table was a heavy oak podium which was situated much too high for me to use.

"Would a couple of you gentlemen please put this podium on the floor for me as I can't move it?" I asked. Nobody moved.

"I am sorry there are no gentlemen here, I will just wait until two of you agree to move this for me," I said. "I can't move it."

Finally, two men straggled up to the front and moved it for me.

> *"She was a redhead.*
>
> *"It was Ken McKirdy who knew of Ruth so, with his advice, Ruth was hired to teach political science. As an arts faculty we would be selling political science as an elective to the Faculty of Engineering. It was Ruth's challenge to generate enthusiasm for the course. At the same time, she was Dean at Renison College. While I didn't have close contact with that part of her responsibilities, she was a going concern.*
>
> *"Her strength, as a teacher, was her personality; it was her nature to reach out to people in conversation. Even today, when she dines with our friends, she is the centre of banter and fun and on occasion, pseudo-debates. It comes naturally. When she gets a notion, she is confident in her own slant on the subject matter. That is close to the red-head business."*
>
> *Paul Cornell*

Many of my students didn't appreciate the link between political science and their careers until I underlined the relationship between their field of study and the inevitable connection to politics by emphasizing the importance of getting

BE A "NICE" GIRL!

along with municipal politicians. I reminded them that as engineers, they would be building roads and bridges which were matters of great interest to politicians. I also stressed the use of good grammar, an area in which engineers were traditionally weak.

Essays were an important element of the course. I tried to present practical topics to help them relate the study of engineering to political science. Two students, in particular, didn't like any of the proposed essay topics so we talked about a number of other possibilities. They decided to examine the political aspects of creating the Trans-Canada pipeline. I borrowed a set of the House of Commons Parliamentary debates from another university for them because they weren't available yet at Waterloo. The two students produced an excellent essay.

At the end of the school year, my colleague in political science, Terry Qualter, his wife Shirley and I went to a local pub frequented by students. All of a sudden, three or four mugs of beer appeared in front of me. I turned to Terry and asked him why he had ordered that quantity of beer.

"You know I can't drink that much beer!"

"I didn't order it. I had nothing to do with it," Terry replied.

"Did you order it Shirley?" I asked.

"No," she said.

I called the waiter back to tell him I hadn't ordered the beer and couldn't possibly drink it. The waiter pointed to four young engineering students who were sitting nearby and waving at me.

A politician to a political scientist: "Will you marry me?"

The PC Party was of great interest to me even as I taught at Waterloo. I was delighted to accept an invitation from Elizabeth Jansen Dreger, the Conservative Women of Canada's President who also lived in Waterloo, to represent the constituency as a delegate at the PC's annual meeting at the Chateau Laurier in Ottawa.

Another chapter of my life was about to begin. It was a Friday in January of 1963. Elizabeth and I were staying at the Lord Elgin Hotel which meant we had a short but brisk walk to the Chateau Laurier. One of the first people I met was an old acquaintance who had just been appointed the 20th Lieutenant-Governor of Ontario, the Hon. Earl Rowe. After I congratulated him on his appointment, I gave him a good-natured scolding for attending a political meeting when he was supposed to be non-partisan. Earl invited me for drinks and dinner because he wanted me to meet his daughter, Jean Casselman, who was also an MP. When I declined because I was traveling with Elizabeth, Earl insisted she attend as well.

As luck would have it, our first official date was captured on film. Dick and I chat with Thomas Mulvagh and his wife at the PC's annual meeting at the Chateau Laurier in 1963.

As we entered Earl's suite, Jean was sitting on the sofa. She was holding hands with a Cabinet Minister whom I knew by reputation, but had not met. Jean's date was the Hon. R.A. (Dick) Bell. After dinner at the Canadian Grill, about 20 of us enjoyed the dance band. Dick leaned over to explain he wasn't going to ask me to dance because he didn't dance. I remember thinking there was no reason for Dick to ask me because he was with his girl friend. Before the night was over, Dick invited all of us to dinner the next night.

In a chance meeting in the hall on Saturday afternoon, Dick asked me to join him for drinks with some senior PC members before dinner. Dick wasn't a very good dancer, but he did ask me to dance that night. I returned to Waterloo on Sunday. On Monday, he telephoned to say he was traveling through Waterloo, en route to Stratford for a political engagement, and he wanted to have dinner with me Friday evening. In the course of the conversation, Dick asked me if I would consider marrying him. "No thank you. I like my job and I don't want to get married," I replied, but I did accept the dinner invitation at Walper House in Kitchener. On his way back Saturday evening, he dropped in to see me. He was carrying a hamper containing two glasses and a bottle of champagne. Five dates later, we met at the altar.

It was kind of nice to think someone would want to marry me. I didn't and I don't have many close friends. I was glad to find someone who was interested in what concerned me. Dick loved me and I think he was rather proud of me. He was an attractive man and a man of the finest integrity. We were older than most people who married. We both knew what it was like to be lonely and I think we knew what was important to both of us. We were interested in the same things, we loved to travel and politics was our passion.

One evening, Dick took great pains to tell me about his financial situation. Security was a serious matter for me. I was a middle-aged widow who was just starting a new career with no pension.

Much later, I learned Dick went home after the annual meeting and told his daughter, Judy, he had met someone he wanted to marry. Judy was surprised because Dick had promised her he would never marry after her mother died. Judy, who was articling as a lawyer, was his hostess and ran his house. It took some time, but Judy and I became friends.

Dick and I selected an engagement ring in Toronto in February, but I didn't wear it because we wanted to keep it a secret for a while. I didn't hesitate to tell Bill's mother about my plans because time and again, Maidie had urged me to remarry. She was very concerned that I would be very lonely if I didn't. When I asked her to come to the wedding at Waterloo, initially she declined.

"Oh no, no, I couldn't do that."

"Well, I wish you would consider it. Doris, my bridesmaid, will take you to the wedding."

"Oh no, I couldn't do that," she said and in the same breath, "What should I wear?"

"Who are you marrying?"

"I can't tell you right now because you would know who he was and I just don't want you to gossip all over the place," I replied. Maidie belonged to a bridge club and a bowling club.

"Aren't you going to tell me?"

"Well, not just now."

"Is he an Anglican?"

"Yes."

"Good. Is he a Conservative?"

"Yes."

"Alright then. It is okay." She came to the wedding. Maidie loved Dick and we continued to be the best of friends, visiting back and forth, until her death in the 1970s.

We had one other minor detail to work out. I needed to change my name on my passport. When I sent the passport to Dick, who was the Federal Minister of Citizenship and Immigration, he was horrified. He hadn't realized I was an American citizen. Fortunately, a new passport was issued without delay because of my length of residency in Canada and the fact I had acquired landed immigrant status 20 years earlier.

Dick was working hard on his 1963 federal re-election bid as we prepared for our wedding. I was watching the televised election results at Peggy and Paul Cornell's home when Dick telephoned to tell me the marriage was off.

"I am being defeated. I can't ask you to marry a failure," he explained.

By this time, I had resigned my position at Waterloo and our wedding date was set.

"I am not marrying you because you are a Cabinet minister or because you are a member of Parliament. If you want to call it off, that is your prerogative. Just make sure you know why you are calling it off," I replied.

Our engagement was announced on the front page of the Ottawa Citizen's April 10, 1963 edition. Richard Albert Bell and I were married on a bright, sunny day at 11 a.m. on May 4, 1963 at the Church of the Holy Saviour in Waterloo, Ontario by Rev. Denton Massey. Renison College's Chaplain Rev. Morley Pinkney celebrated communion.

The local *Kitchener-Waterloo Record's* headline proclaimed: *"Loses Cabinet post but wins girl's hand"* One newspaper's headline announced *"Lost vote but won a bride"* and another suggested I was the "consolation" prize.

I was given in marriage by long-time friend John J. Denison, Deputy General Manager of the Toronto-Dominion Bank. The Hon. Ernie Halpenny was Dick's best man. Doris Chappell was my bridesmaid for the second time. I wore a street-length dress of pale blue chiffon and lace, and carried a bouquet of white orchids and yellow roses.

After we signed the register in the vestry, the Minister invited Dick to kiss the bride. I turned to Dick waiting for my kiss and expecting him to say something sentimental. Instead I heard, "Where the hell are your glasses?" Both my Aunt Dorothy and Doris, my bridesmaid, had suggested I not wear my glasses during the wedding. I obliged.

Dick and I were married by Denton Massey, a great friend of Dick's. Originally, Denton was a United Church member who had gained a reputation for hosting inspirational bible classes at Maple Leaf Gardens

The Kitchener-Waterloo Record *announces our wedding with the headline: Lost Cabinet post but wins girl s hand.* (Kitchener-Waterloo Record)

during the 1930s. He was related to Vincent and Raymond Massey. Denton served as an air force officer during WWII, and at an age when most people retire, he was ordained an Anglican priest and assigned to my church in Waterloo—the Church of the Holy Saviour.

Dick and Denton immediately recognized each other at a service we were attending there. That fortuitous encounter settled where we were going to be married and resolved a predicament. I wanted to be married in the Anglican Church but Dick's interest had waned when the Church had refused to solemnize Dick's marriage to his first wife Winifred, a divorcée. After our marriage, Dick was persuaded to return to church with help from a very sensitive and sympathetic Rector Bill Belford of Christ Church in Bells Corners—the church where Dick's father and grandfather had served as wardens. On our first Easter, Dick gave me a prayer book.

When we signed the marriage register, Denton presented us with the *Book of Common Prayer* in which he wrote: "To two very special people, Dick and Ruth, in sincere devotion and with prayer, for their happiness. Dent 1963."

Following our wedding, we invited our guests to lunch in the Crystal Ballroom at Walper House. We spent the night at Niagara Falls, boarded a plane the next

When Dick and I boarded the Prinses Irene *to return to Canada, the crew recognized me from the trip I had made from Australia after Bill s death. (m.s.* Prinses Irene, *Oranje Lijn (Mij. Zeetransport) N.V., Rotterdam)*

day in Toronto, and enjoyed the next six weeks in Europe touring Portugal, Spain, Italy, Austria, Scotland and England.

Our decision to return home by ship was made one day as we walked down Piccadilly in London. I noticed a shipping line office.

"Oh look," I said to Dick. "That's the *Prinses Irene*. That's the freighter I took home to Canada on my way back from Australia, nine years ago!

"Would you like to go home by ship?" Dick asked. Of course, that was fine with me. He tried to book passage on a passenger ship but nothing was available, even with the intervention of our High Commissioner George Drew. So we took the *Prinses Irene* home. As our barge approached the freighter, some of the officers were leaning over the railing as they waited for us. Suddenly, several of them yelled, "Oh, Mrs. Rolph, Mrs. Rolph, how nice to see you!" They remembered me.

Shortly after Dick and I made our home at *Fairfields*, the Bell homestead in Nepean, the Privy Council hosted a dinner to celebrate our marriage. There were quite a few speeches, lots of politicians, and plenty of wine. I knew many of the people because of my work with the PC Party including Monty Monteith, Gordon Churchill, George Nowland, Jim MacDonnell and Don Flemming. Dick was alarmed when I was asked to say a few words. I don't recall what I said but there were a few more speeches before they finally called on the groom. I can still see Dick standing up at the dinner table and I only remember his concluding remarks: "...and I hope you will all agree that a politician and a political scientist make good bedfellows!"

Not everyone was happy about our marriage. I would say I was accepted with mixed feelings. Don Morrow, an MPP and one of Dick's political friends, chastised me for ruining Dick's political career because I was purportedly a

Roman Catholic who had married an Anglican. I asked Don how he had come to understand I was a Roman Catholic.

"You were married at 11 a.m. and only Roman Catholics marry at that time in the morning!" he replied.

"You have made an assumption, in error." I countered. "We are both Anglicans, not that that makes any difference."

To some, I was an outsider. Several women thought Dick should have married within his constituency. Perhaps they had their eye him because he was an eligible widower of some

Holly and Sandhurst joined me in this photo taken at Fairfields. (John Evans Photography)

means. On the other hand, Dick's constituents presented us with a beautiful silver tray as a wedding gift. We also enjoyed a good rapport with Nepean Township staff which continues today. The Township had retained Bell, Baker to provide legal advice and representation. When Dick took sick later in life, Nepean's C.M. (Merv) Beckstead, David E. Hobbs and W.T. (Bill) Leathem were very supportive.

During the first year of our marriage, I registered at Carleton University in three graduate courses and three extra courses—required for women who had worked and studied part-time at night. Four were seminars on political sociology and the political process, two on Canadian government—one at the national level and the other at the municipal level; and a fifth focused on Commonwealth governments. I also was learning how to drive a car—my beloved Acadian which I named *Evangeline*—run a house and a garden. I didn't know a weed from a flower! I attended many of the sales and annual meetings hosted by PC women's groups in Carleton Riding. That was the wife's job in those days. The level of involvement is quite different today.

I kept a copy of a letter I wrote to a friend in February of 1964, parts of which I will share with you because it will give you a sense of our life in the early days.

"Our social life is also quite active. Last week, we went to the Press Club Ball, which was a success. I even did the twist with an old newspaper acquaintance, the *Times of London* correspondent. Dick and I attended a 50th wedding anniversary party on Sunday (Dick is kept busy attending such affairs and I tag along to be looked over by all the old girls.) Next week is the opening of Parliament. Dick has never been to one, except as a Commoner, behind the bar of the Senate. So this time, we go as a Privy Councillor and wife. In the middle of the afternoon, we turn up in full evening dress, and sit in the Senate, after which we go to receptions given by the Speakers of the Senate and Commons, followed by dinner at the Rideau Club. The previous evening, we go to a state reception at Government House, which will probably be dull, but I must go at least once. I am so excited about having two evening dresses, that I must tell you. For the G.G.'s reception, I will wear a midnight blue, re-embroidered lace dress with green and gold shoes, and my jade and sapphire jewellery. For the opening, I will wear a pale yellow-flecked, long, slim silk skirt, slit up the side, with one shoulder bare. The bodice and front of the over-jacket (must be decent) is made of the same silk, only embroidered in gold. Judy's dressmaker is doing it for me and the first fitting augers well. Since we are going to a couple of other balls this month, the dresses will be used again.…

"In addition, there are many political meetings. In Carleton constituency, there are 11 (count 'em) women's associations and they all want to see their beloved Dick and to inspect his bride. So tonight and Thursday, we are off to two of those and some more next week. The main executive numbers over 200. I thought I had had them all to dinner when we had 24 to a buffet before Christmas, but now Dick tells me, we must entertain the entire executive and wives at some kind of do (200, whew). He is getting ready for the next election, for everybody seems to be mad at the Liberals and are finding out their current member is not very effective. In fact, there seems to be general disappointment with the Liberal Government. It's only the thought of another election, when we have had four in six years, that deters the people, I think."

Learning about political life was interesting although, not always pleasant; in fact, some elections were pretty nasty. That being said, I liked political life because I met many fascinating people. Dick, who was a Red Tory, was elected as MP for Carleton Riding as part of the PC's minority government win in 1957. Dick was re-elected in the 1958 Conservative landslide, which produced the greatest majority of seats in Canadian history, and served that term as Parliamentary-Secretary to the Minister of Finance. Following the 1962 election of a Conservative minority government, Dick was appointed to the Privy Council as Minister of Citizenship and Immigration. In 1963, the Conservatives were defeated. Dick lost by 1,157 votes to Lloyd Francis. The 1963 defeat was pretty dreadful. Dick was heartbroken. I don't blame him because he had devoted most of his life to politics. His political tides would turn in 1965.

Dick was a rather serious person with a droll sense of humour. He was a man of the finest integrity and he had very, very strict rules of conduct for himself. I remember one particular incident in which Dick and NDP leader David Lewis were being interviewed by the CBC. Dick declined an honorarium for his appearance because he already was being paid as an MP. He was quite irked when David accepted it.

My husband was a man of great loyalty. He received his first degree from the University of Toronto in 1934 and his barrister-at-law degree in 1938—the only degree a lawyer received then. Dick was described by his peers as an intellectual lawyer.

His affiliation with the PCs began when he was in his teens. In the late 1930s, he became the PCs first professional party organizer. He became executive director of the Progressive Conservative Party of Canada when George Drew was Leader. Five or six years later, he decided to work full-time on his law practice and part-time for the PC Party. He served in John Diefenbaker's Cabinet and he worked very hard to get Bob Stanfield elected as the federal PC Leader. When the opportunity presented itself, Bob appointed him to two or three parliamentary commissions. Dick was a member of the Ontario Law Reform Commission for more than 20 years and was awarded the Law Society of Upper Canada's first Distinguished Service Medal, posthumously.

Dick shared a common interest in agriculture with many of his constituents who earned their living by farming. Three generations of Bells before him had been prosperous dairy farmers, and his father and grandfather were active in municipal politics. It was not surprising that Dick embraced public life or that he had such a good relationship with the rural community. On many occasions he would drive out to the country to meet farmers and tend to their legal affairs and when he needed someone to witness wills, he would ask me to accompany him.

I know only what a wife knows. Apparently, Dick was an excellent lawyer who was very good in municipal matters. He was very thoughtful and considerate in his business relationships. He was a wonderful husband. As soon as he discovered that I could manage financial affairs, I had his complete confidence. I think we had mutual faith in one another. We were interested in the same things. We liked traveling and we enjoyed many trips together. We had similar bereavements. We had a lot in common.

Managing my personal and professional responsibilities together with completing my graduate thesis on *Conservative Party Leadership Conventions* was a juggling act, to say the least. In preparing my thesis, I knew some of the research material could be found in the bowels of PC headquarters on Laurier Avenue. My first challenge was the basement—it was a hell hole. I burrowed around in a tunnel leading to the furnace room. I wasn't prepared for what I found. Among the unrecorded artifacts was a poster developed for Sir John A. Macdonald's last campaign: *"The old Flag, the old Policy and the old Leader"* and the organizational papers for the first Liberal-Conservative Party National Convention in Canada in 1927. I was thrilled to find these treasures. They were invaluable as research for me. Some people would not be the least bit interested in archives and would have thrown out the material just as easily. From my perspective, if others were to enjoy them, a permanent home was absolutely imperative to the preservation of these links to our Canadian heritage.

At the time, I didn't know of one good book on political parties in Canada. Many political biographies had been written but nothing had been published on the history of our Parties. I persuaded the PC Women's Association to establish Canada's first political library as our 1967 Centennial project. We had a crew of volunteers including such young men as Joe Clark who was President of the Young Conservatives, and Art Donohue. I called in as many parliamentary wives and colleagues as I could to help. We dusted off, sorted and organized old records and files and a fundraising campaign was launched. The Macdonald-Cartier Library, which consisted of a library and an archive, was opened in the new PC Headquarters at 178 Queen Street by the Hon. Robert Stanfield, as one of his first public acts after taking his Commons seat in November, 1967. The library's name is an enduring remembrance of the alliance between Sir John A. Macdonald and Sir George-Étienne Cartier during a pivotal point in Canada's earlier nation-building years. The Macdonald-Cartier Library was used as a reading room and housed Parliamentary guides, portraits of the leaders, and other volumes of Canadian political history. Sir John A. Macdonald's desk and a desk set belonging to Sir Robert Borden were on display.

I arranged to have the PC papers deposited with the National Archives. We were the first political party to do so. The Liberals and the New Democratic Party followed suit.

> *"Ruth Bell demonstrated a deep commitment to preserving and protecting the history of the Progressive Conservative Party—a Party that has been around longer than this country.*
>
> *"She realized the archives of the Party were in jeopardy and made it her priority to resurrect and protect them in a permanent way. That is her legacy to the Party."*
>
> *The Hon. David S. H. MacDonald*

Chronicles of events and decisions are important assets to any organization. Without properly archiving these records, you don't have a history. You can't know where you are going until you know where you have been. Vincent Massey put it this way: "What's past is present. What's present is the prologue."

Over the years, I have tried to demonstrate a commitment to the preservation of archives of organizations in which I have been involved. During 1975-1976, I pushed to have the records of the Canadian Federation of University Women (CFUW), the National Council of Women (NCW) and those of other women's groups deposited as collections within National Archives of Canada. I believed that Canadians ought to have the ability to access records dealing with the advancement of the status of women during International Women's Year in 1975 and beyond.

Mary Maclaren and I took it a step further by enrolling in a 14-part archives course sponsored by the Archivists Association of Ontario in the 1980s. Ours was the first graduating class and I was proud to be valedictorian. Since then, I have served as archivist for several voluntary organizations including the Queensway Carleton Hospital Volunteers, CFUW, NCW, Ottawa Council of Women, and as first president of the Friends of the Archives of the Anglican Diocese of Ottawa.

A respect for archives was a family passion. Dick was instrumental in ensuring sufficient funds were available to construct the National Archives and Library when he was Minister of Citizenship and Immigration. His ministerial papers are deposited there as are our personal papers. I would be so pleased if a student were to research Dick's story because he played a significant role in political life in Canada.

The year of the alphabet: M.A., Mrs., and MP

1965 was the year of the alphabet in the Bell household. I received my M.A., Judy got her Mrs., and Dick regained his MP.

I was quite pleased when I received my Masters in Political Science on Friday, May 21, 1965 from Carleton University. Dick was very supportive, I was older and wiser and my thesis on *Conservative Party Conventions 1927-1956* was well-received.

The materials I unearthed at the PC Headquarters were vital to relating the history of the various stages of devolution of authority within the Party from the appointment of the PC leader by the Governor General to election by convention based on popular representation. My thesis expounded on the various selection processes and procedures that superseded the Governor General's appointment of the Conservatives' great chieftain, Sir John A. Macdonald who achieved the role of leadership (1867-1891) by his pre-eminence as a politician and parliamentarian rather than by formal election. Naturally, the new approaches—the Cabinet/Parliamentary Caucus system, the initiation of special devices such as the preferential ballot by Cabinet in 1920, the use of the convention in 1927, 1938, 1942, 1948, and 1956 and a modified convention-caucus combination in 1941—spawned new issues.

Excerpts follow of some of the contemporary arguments I raised about the use of conventions and the accelerated role of the mass media which continue to generate similar discussion and debate today.

"In 1942, there was no opportunity for the build-up of a potential candidate. The full slate of candidates was not known until the last minute, thereby confining the opinion-forming period mostly to the convention days. The burden of making decisions fell mostly to the delegates.

"In contrast, during the 1956 convention, the party hierarchy was almost unanimously opposed to John Diefenbaker, but there was no strong enthusiasm for anyone else. The powers that the hierarchy may have had were dissipated in the unsuccessful search for an alternate candidate. It was left in the position of being unable to withstand the strong sentiment built up over the years for the successful

Dick was very supportive and I was quite pleased when I received my Masters in Political Science from Carleton University.

candidate. Combined with his popular support, was the view widely held by party members that Mr. Diefenbaker was the only man who could, at this point in history, lead the Conservative Party to long-desired political power.

"This underlines the role in which public opinion fostered and developed by the mass media can play in a convention. What were the impacts of increased radio coverage and the introduction of television broadcasts? To what extent is news reported and news created? The flow of stories in the news media that Mr. X may be a candidate, that he made a speech here and there, and that he is likely to win, contributes to the public sentiment to get on the bandwagon and support Mr. X. This general view is imposed on delegates even before they become delegates. It affects their ability to make objective judgments on the merits of the various candidates. Further questions may be asked for which no answer is readily available. To what extent will the delegates be captive of the public opinion environment created by the mass media and to what extent will he or she be able to exercise his or her independent judgment? Has the convention become the imprimatur of authority or is the legitimacy, upon which public decisions are made, already informally reached?"

Looking at today's situation, the role of the news media at the recent Liberal Party leadership convention in November 2003 was limited to Paul Martin hype. There was no competition of ideas or choice of leaders. Instead, we had two evenings of entertainment. It is the only convention, in my memory, where there was only one plausible candidate. That doesn't give you much choice.

Thoughtful discussions and intellectual debates on party policy, once a primary function of the convention, have been replaced with loud bands and balloons, and a competition for the largest group of demonstrators. Conventions have become entertainment events. Moreover, broadcasting the results of advance polling to inform voters which Party or leader is leading going into an election, sadly, can and does influence delegates and voters who haven't taken the time to decipher the differences.

Recently, I was watching the Saskatchewan election results. John Courtney, a professor of political science at the University of Saskatchewan, was one of the commentators. It brought back many memories. John had come to Ottawa, some years previously, to research voting, elections and means of voting. When he discovered my thesis covered similar issues, he used it for research purposes.

I was delighted to be asked by Eugene Forsey to teach courses on Federalism and the Canadian Government—a career I pursued from the mid-1960s until the 1970s. Eugene was a very distinguished man, the director of research for the Canadian Labour Congress and an expert on Canadian constitutional history at Carleton University. Eugene had experienced the political arena, personally, as a CCF candidate who ran unsuccessfully against George Drew in Carleton Riding in 1949.

It was my responsibility to organize discussion groups headed by teaching assistants. When Eugene was away, I took over his classes. I also taught courses on Canadian Government at St. Patrick's College before it became part of Carleton University, and a beginner's course on Canadian politics and government at Algonquin College.

As a university lecturer, I encouraged young people to come and talk to me about careers. I urged students, particularly first year students, to keep an open mind about their studies, and to try everything they could without interfering with their education. Dick's daughter, Judy, knew what she wanted to do at the age of 10. Some people don't. Judging from my own experience, I took the courses I had to take and in the course of sampling things, I completely changed my studies. I advised students to learn how to be organized, how to evaluate courses of action, and recommended that they participate in the drama club, public speaking, sports and other undergraduate activities. I assumed students knew the fundamentals such as being honest, pleasant and punctual.

"Ruth, who was always thirsting for knowledge, was very much in evidence as a participant in the sessions moderated by her husband Bill. She reminded us on more than one occasion that she was not a university graduate. Some university wives were condescending. They knew the answer but they asked the question anyway. Ruth showed them because after Bill died, she obtained her B.A. and her M.A. largely through evening studies. That is a good indication of Ruth's determination and her thirst for knowledge. She is a lifelong learner and that was very much in evidence before her eyesight failed. She would go to Oxford in the summer for six-week residential courses. That determination is very characteristic of Ruth."

John Harrington

A wedding in the family

Judy's wedding in 1965 was another very significant milestone in our lives. Judy was working as a lawyer with Fraser & Beattie Barristers & Solicitors in Toronto when she announced her plans to marry Gerald Oyen. She returned to Fairfields one weekend to discuss the wedding plans.

"Ruth will go to Toronto with you to shop for your trousseau, and she will select your clothing, and arrange the wedding," Dick announced to Judy and me.

"I am not going to do that," I replied. "I am not going to tell her what to do and I am not going to tell her what to wear. She is 25 years—old and she knows what she likes. If she wants my advice, I will be happy to provide it." At Judy's request, I went to Toronto as her consultant to help her select her linens and such.

Judy developed the guest list for the wedding at Christ Church in Bells Corners and I helped her to arrange the reception in the gardens at *Fairfields*. Judy wanted champagne imported from France and a chocolate wedding cake. I had some trouble arranging the cake but I did. We had a chocolate cake for the bride and a traditional fruit cake for the groom. As for the champagne, the bridal party had French champagne and the rest of us enjoyed an excellent Canadian brand.

Judy returned to Bell, Baker to practise law when she and her husband relocated to Ottawa. Dick came home one day and announced, "Ruth, you have got to talk to Judy. Her skirts are just too short to wear to the office and she wears too much make-up. You have to tell her!"

"I will not. She is your daughter and a member of your firm. If you have any concerns about her appearance, then you, as the head of the law firm, should discuss it with her!" I retorted. That ended the conversation.

Dick, Judy and I spent many Christmases together at Montebello, in the Barbados, and at *Fairfields*. Dick usually made the reservations. Unfortunately, he left it so late one year that we didn't get trip confirmation until the last minute. Judy and I decided to book the reservations in January for our next Christmas vacation, and we also agreed not to tell him until he went to make the arrangements. Well, Dick was absolutely furious. In a way, the "booking incident" helped bring Judy and me closer together. She was a very sensitive person.

I had one unfortunate accident while holidaying in Bequia in the West Indies' Grenadines. The night before we were to return to Canada, I went to shut the door in our unit to keep the rain out. I slipped on the ceramic floor, hit my head and broke my wrist. Dick chartered a plane to St. Vincent. Unfortunately, the hospital's emergency department was closed on Sunday. It wasn't until I arrived home that my wrist was put into a cast. Some days later, I had a check-up scheduled. Dick came home to help me get ready. I couldn't do anything with the one wrist which made putting panty hose on a particularly, difficult task. In those days, women didn't wear pants as a rule. Dick was down on his knees, struggling to help me put my panty hose on, and I was shouting, "No. No. You don't do it that way. You do it this way!" He was getting exasperated. Finally, Dick looked up at me and said, "You ought to be damn glad I don't know how to put these things on!"

Judy, Dick and I could carry on a conversation that would cover just about every hospital issue in Ottawa. At one point, Dick was the president of the Queensway Carleton Hospital Board of Directors, Judy was president of the Civic Hospital Board of Directors and a member of the Ottawa-Carleton Regional District Health Council, and I was a member of Royal Ottawa Hospital's Board of Directors. Dick worked hard to ensure the western region including Nepean had its own hospital. It took several tries, but he succeeded with a group of like-minded community activists including Reeve Aubrey Moodie.

Hell-bent for election

Dick came home one day to tell me he had been asked to present a paper at the Commonwealth Law Conference meeting in Sydney, Australia. Canada's 27th federal general election was expected to be called and when it was, Dick and I experienced a hair-raising trip back to Canada which he dubbed *Hell-bent for Election*.

Our trip started out innocently.

"How would you feel about going back to Australia? Would that upset you?" Dick asked.

I thought that was very considerate question because it would be my first trip back since Bill's death. As it happened, the International Federation of University Women was meeting in Brisbane, Australia, just days before Dick's conference. It was a great opportunity to visit some of my old friends in Canberra who were glad to meet Dick. On that particular trip, we traveled to Fiji, New Zealand, Brisbane, Sydney, Adelaide and Darwin in Australia and on to Singapore, Hong Kong, Taiwan, Japan and Vancouver.

We were in Japan when the election was called and we needed all the help we could get to return to Canada immediately. Part of our harrowing adventure is described aptly by John Harrington who was a student of my first husband, Bill.

"My wife and I arrived in Tokyo in August of 1965. I was a counsellor at the Canadian Embassy. At that time, Dick and Ruth were attending the Commonwealth Law Conference in Australia which must have been rather poignant for Ruth as the first trip back since Bill's death. She knew we were in Tokyo so she let us know they were planning a week's holidays in Japan. I recommended a lovely, mountain resort called Hakone at the Highland Hotel. It had a full Scottish atmosphere, complete with tartans.

"The Bells were concerned that an election might be called in Canada and they would be incommunicado, so I agreed to let them know if this did occur. Within 24 hours, the election call was made, prompting my call to the Bells. They hopped on the train to Tokyo and arrived a few hours later in their holiday clothes. Timing was of the essence. I took the ambassador's car and driver and met the Bells at the train station. A police escort, complete with screaming sirens, rushed us through the Tokyo traffic. The traffic in late afternoon was pretty horrendous—solid gridlock—at least it was then. We arrived at the airport where CPA was holding the flight. Dick and Ruth were still in their holiday clothes when they got back to Ottawa."

John Harrington

Our trip to the airport was accomplished at break-neck speed, but John didn't know about the first leg of our terrifying trip to catch the train to Tokyo until later. We were having lunch in the mountains when we received John's telephone call. Our Japanese hosts organized a taxi to take us through the mountains to Hakone to pick up our luggage. We were to continue by taxi to board the bullet train to Tokyo. We were scared to death as the taxi hurtled along the mountainous roads because were we to have an accident, no one would ever find us. We didn't speak Japanese and the taxi driver didn't speak English. We were petrified, but we arrived at the train station…shaken but safe. As we boarded, I noticed a little café on the train. When I asked Dick if he wanted a beverage, he asked for a stiff scotch. My request for a cup of tea and a whiskey was interpreted as two whiskey teas. Dick wasn't too enthralled with the concoction. We arrived in Vancouver, looking tired and somewhat dishevelled in our holiday clothes—tops and shorts, dirty white socks and running shoes.

BE A *"NICE"* GIRL!

Dick's 1965 election campaign was the first one in which I took part. Quite a number of young people from the Civic Hospital's Nursing School and the university volunteered to help him at his headquarters. He would never let me go door-to-door unless one of them accompanied me.

One night when we returned home, we were quite footsore and weary. Seldom did we canvass together because we covered more territory by going our separate ways. We hadn't had supper yet and I was resting. Dick didn't take a drink during an election campaign but he offered me one. I accepted, but not before I told him, "I had no idea when I married you that you were going to turn me into a street-walker!" We laughed about that.

Dick didn't want me to be involved in running the office or the campaign. I was a front which was fine with me. I had to turn up at every meeting and sit there like a dutiful wife and not applaud him. Those were strict instructions. You don't applaud your own spouse. Now, I know that is not true in other cases, but it was true in our family!

Dick would talk things over with me to obtain my views on different issues. It was my job to answer the phone calls from constituents to our home. His office was quite small and employed two or three people.

"Grateful" was how I would describe the feelings I had for people like Jean Pigott and Grete Hale who would bring us a hamper of food so I wouldn't have to worry about dinner on a campaign night. Other people were thoughtful in various ways. Taking care of the husband was the wife's job. She was to see that dinner was ready, the poor husband got his rest, and somehow or other, his shirts were laundered. My mother used to say that she could have been a more successful businesswoman if only she had had a househusband.

Many supporters would have functions at their homes. Intimate social life was limited but I made some very nice friends. Dick had lots of supporters. He was much admired and he also had good friends such as Lon Campbell and J.C and Jean Horowitz and Township of Nepean staff. Lots of people were friends. Years later, we continue to be glad to see one another.

People weren't as busy then as they are now. They didn't watch as much television; they didn't have as many other activities. It just seems to me that we rush around more now than we did then. Whether it is because I am getting older and less able to run, I don't know. But, when the election came, people came in droves to support their candidate. Whether they do that now, I cannot say because I am not in touch.

In 1965, the Liberals won, but Dick regained his seat, winning by a margin of 933 votes. I wore a deep blue silk dress to one of Dick's first functions—a dress I had purchased just before we raced home from Tokyo.

The electoral district of Carleton was abolished in 1966 and redistributed into two ridings: Grenville-Carleton and Ottawa West. At one point, it was suggested Dick run in one riding and I run in the next one. He ran but I didn't. I couldn't stand the guff, the hurt, or the criticism that goes with politics. In fact, I thought one politician in the house was enough. In those days, the politician's wife did a lot of things that spouses don't do today. I became a specialist in opening bazaars.

The 1968 federal election was a different story. Robert Stanfield was the new leader of the PC Party during a period of time defined by *Trudeaumania*. Canadians were mesmerized by Pierre Elliott Trudeau, the new leader of the Liberal Party. On the eve of the election, Dick and I were listening to the news. It was a turning point for the Liberals. It happened at the St. Jean Baptiste Day Parade in Montreal which Pierre Trudeau was watching from a reviewing stand. A riot broke out nearby. Pierre was escorted away but not before the cameras showed Pierre staring down the rioters. Dick correctly announced "We have lost the election." Pierre Trudeau led the Liberals to a majority government and served as Prime Minister from 1968 to 1979 and from 1980 to 1984. People said later, "Bob Stanfield was the best Prime Minister Canada never had." Dick ran against Lloyd Francis in the Ottawa West Riding and lost. Dick was very, very upset and depressed when he lost the election. He planned to return to his law practice but it took him a while to get up enough gumption to go. He was asked, once, to stand for leader of the party, but he declined. I don't think he had any ambitions that way, but he liked being a Member of Parliament and he was a good one. He did the very best for his constituents. I continue to meet people today who speak highly of him as an MP and Minister.

Dick's law partner, Walter Baker, regained that seat in 1972 and held it for four consecutive elections until his death in 1983. During that time, the riding was renamed Nepean-Carleton.

The reality of politics

This is a photo of some members of John Diefenbaker's Cabinet. Back row from left are: unidentified, Wallace McCutcheon, Dick Bell, Michael Starr, George Nowland, unidentified, Alvin Hamilton, Ernest Halpenny, Walter Dinsdale, Marcel Lambert, Fred McGee, unidentified, J.W. Monteith. Front row from left are: Gordon Churchill, Léon Balcer, J.M. McDonnell, Prime Minister Diefenbaker, Don Flemming and Davey Fulton. (National Film Board Photo)

From my vantage point, I have viewed politics from the perspective of a researcher for the PC Party, as the wife of a politician, and as a teacher of political science. Teaching political science is a far cry from living the reality of politics.

Not surprisingly, the amalgamation of the PC Conservative Party and the Canadian Alliance into the new Conservative Party is of great interest to me. Media coverage of issues often includes commentary from professors of political science. Professors make very useful comments, but they don't know the nitty-gritty details.

Politics is down-to-earth, hand-to-hand, and face-to-face. You do what you think is best. You have to be courteous, polite, and you need to listen. Dick was a very good listener. I learned to listen.

The practical experience I gained working for the PC Party was not covered in textbooks. That's why, I think I was a good teacher and that's why I was hired at Waterloo. They had heard I had worked on the Nova Scotia election campaign as well as several by-elections, and they knew I was experienced in analyzing election results and in recording party policy and its development.

As Dick's wife, I learned about people's personal problems in relation to the national economy. It brings it home to you when you talk about health care in one breath and in the next, you are confronted with a family struggling with a very serious health care problem. It is the difference between the microcosm and the macrocosm. Politics is about individuals. Theory is about theory.

A political wife was a little like a decoration. Margaret Trudeau likened it to being a rose in her husband's lapel. Maryon Pearson made a similar statement earlier. You sit up on a platform and you don't say a word, or you say very little. You turn up at meetings and you walk the streets as the partner of the candidate. You subjugate your own personality and your own life. As a spouse, I had to be friendly and have the ability to cover up for Dick when I sensed he should know the person, but didn't. I didn't make it a public issue that I was teaching at the university. My profession frightened some people in those days. If people asked, I told them. I don't think people are as intimidated by the profession today. But this was 40 years ago.

Wives were just beginning to enter the workforce in serious numbers. Wives were supposed to be the supporting person in a political person's life. I enjoyed the Parliamentary Wives' Association and met some very nice women from all the parties. I didn't always enjoy the individual women's association meetings and talking about grandchildren. I like to hear about my friends' grandchildren but it is not a prime focus. Being a wife wasn't a secondary role but you were not Ruth Bell. In those days, you were Mrs. Dick Bell. If you did have a career of your own, you didn't make much of an issue of it. It wasn't too helpful in those days if the wife had a profession or work of her own and couldn't take full part in a campaign.

This stereotyping of women's roles, careers and contributions—which had been simmering for years—was about to become a highly contentious issue.

CHAPTER FOUR

(Colin Price Photo)

Widening the Margins

She who attempts the absurd achieves the impossible

For me, it was clear that the attitudes of men and women toward women had to change, but the challenge would be made more difficult because this way of thinking had economic impacts and legal implications. This challenge, however, was no greater than those faced by past generations or will be faced by future generations.

In my preface, I said I would refer to the achievements of other women because what they did had such a tremendous impact on what I was able to contribute as a person. By acknowledging these women and the way they shaped our society, I believe we gain a better appreciation of what we have today, and what we can achieve as a society by working together.

Our history is rich with many stories of women who persevered to serve their communities as professionals and as politicians. The first woman doctor in Canada, Dr. Emily Howard Stowe, is one example. Dr. Stowe received her medical degree in homeopathy in the late 1860s from the New York Medical College for Women because Canadian medical schools did not accept female students and homeopathy courses were not offered. Eventually, she was licensed in Canada in 1880. She became a founding member of the Toronto Women's Literary Club. Formed in 1876, it was renamed the Canadian Women's Suffrage Association in 1883 to reflect its genuine objective. In 1889, Dr. Stowe helped create yet another pressure group—the Dominion Women's Enfranchisement Association.

Clara Brett Martin was another. She was the first Canadian woman to be admitted as a barrister and solicitor after she fought to have the Law Society of Upper Canada recognize her eligibility in the late 1890s.

In the first half of the 20th century, the general citizenry—men and women— just never thought of women in roles outside of the home. Discrimination existed at different levels. When Agnes Campbell Mcphail of Ontario became the first woman to be elected to Parliament in 1921, the issue was: what would she do for a washroom? A litany of questions followed. Did women need more rest? What happens when women menstruate and they don't think clearly? That was a common comment from men and one which I didn't understand. Perhaps they had difficult wives. Some men alleged women couldn't stand on their feet long enough to carry out a job or an operation. Others wondered whether or not pregnant employees could do their jobs.

The *Famous Five* and the *Persons Case* is another example of how change was brought about when the Federal Government refused to appoint women to the Senate because women weren't persons according to the conventional interpretation of the British North America Act.

This story should be better known because it is one remarkable achievement. The *Persons Case* certainly inspired me to work with others to end systemic discrimination against women and that is why it is included here. As an original member of the committee to select recipients for the Governor General's Awards to Commemorate the *Persons Case*, I was pleased to receive a tastefully arranged collage of photographs of the *Famous Five* at the inaugural ceremony at Rideau Hall. The photos appear on the following page.

The Famous Five and the Persons Case

The *Persons Case* was a watershed event in the 1920s. It set the tone for decades to come. There were many, many more obstacles that would have to be surmounted—through persuasion and legislation—if women were to succeed in achieving equality with men.

A woman was not a person.

At least that was the prevailing interpretation of the British North America Act (1867) until 1929.

But all that changed 75 years ago when the *Famous Five*, a group of five extraordinary women, successfully challenged that definition in a landmark legal appeal known as the *Persons Case*.

The suffrage movement had worked hard to gain women the right to vote as a means of achieving reforms to Prohibition and changes to child welfare and education. The movement caused various Dominion and Provincial Acts to be passed, enabling women to vote and to be candidates. In 1917, women whose husbands or sons were in the military could vote on their behalf. By January 1, 1919, most women were given the right to vote in Federal elections. The exceptions were Asian and Indo-Canadian women and men who gained the right in 1948,

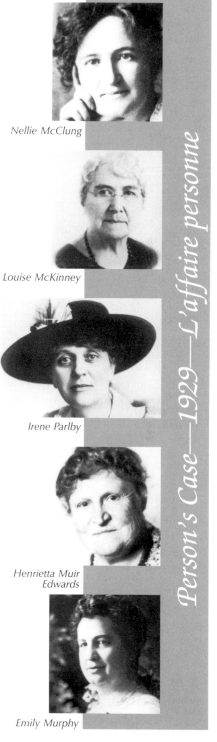

Nellie McClung

Louise McKinney

Irene Parlby

Henrietta Muir Edwards

Emily Murphy

Person's Case—1929—L'affaire personne

some religious groups in 1955, and Aboriginals living on reserves who acquired the right in 1960. By 1927, most women were entitled to vote in Provincial elections with the exception of women in Québec who were disenfranchised until 1940.

The Persons Case removed the remaining legal obstacle in the quest for full participation by women in the Canadian Parliamentary system. Women's groups, led by Emily Murphy, were pressing to have a female appointed to the Canadian Senate. More than 500,000 citizens, including the National Council of Women, signed petitions to support Emily's bid as a person to become a Senator.

Emily had fought and won a similar battle over a woman's status as a person in Alberta's courts. Emily's appointment as the first female police magistrate in the Commonwealth in 1916 was challenged by a lawyer who was presenting a case in her court, on the basis that she was not qualified to perform her duties because she was not a *"person"* according to the British North America Act (BNA) 1867. His premise was based on the view that "women are persons in matters of pain and penalties but are not persons in matters of rights and privileges. Since the office of magistrate is a privilege, the incumbent is here illegally. No decision of hers can be binding."

That hurdle was cleared when a ruling by a Calgary judge which established that both men and women were persons was upheld by the Supreme Court of Alberta. Unfortunately, women's appointments to the Senate continued to be blocked by the Government of Canada's view that the BNA's definition of "qualified person" did not include women.

According to the BNA's Section 24: "The Governor General shall from time to time, in the Queen's name, by instrument under the Great Seal of Canada, summon qualified persons to the Senate; and, subject to the provisions of this Act, every person so summoned shall become and be a member of the Senate and a senator."

At issue was whether the *"persons"* in Section 24 included female persons.

The British North America Act (BNA) of 1867, which set out the powers of the federal and provincial governments, used the word "*persons*" to refer to more than one person and "*he*" when referring to one person. Many held "*he*" to mean only a man could be a person. Groups pressing to have a female person appointed to the Senate of Canada were blocked by that interpretation. If only men were persons, then the only qualified persons, who could be appointed, were men.

Section 23 of the BNA detailed the qualifications for a senator. They included stipulations that *he* must be 30 years of age; *he* must be a natural born subject of the Queen or a subject of the Queen naturalized by a relevant act of parliament or legislature; *he* must own property valued at $4,000 over and above outstanding mortgages or rents, and *he* must possess real and personal property valued at $4,000 over and above debts. Few women met the property requirements.

Moreover, a British Common Law ruling in 1876 had ruled women were eligible "for pains and penalties but not rights and privileges."

In 1927, the *Famous Five*—Emily Murphy, Nellie McClung, Irene Parlby, Louise McKinney and Henrietta Muir Edwards—challenged the Supreme Court of Canada to decide whether women were eligible for appointment to the Senate of Canada.

In the decision, one judge took the view that the word "*persons*" in Section 24 was restricted to males; the other four cited various cases in which women were not permitted to sit or were excluded because of the common law disability of women to hold public office. The Supreme Court of Canada was unanimous in its opinion that women were not persons; therefore women could not be summoned to the Senate.

The *Famous Five* took the *Persons Case* to the highest body of appeal at that time—the Judicial Committee of the Privy Council in Britain. The Judicial Committee, in its decision of October 18, 1929, unanimously ruled that the word *person* in Section 24 included members of the male and the female gender. It held that:

"...*The provisions of the British North America Act, 1867, enacting a constitution for Canada should not be given a narrow and technical construction but a large and liberal interpretation, so that the Dominion to a great extent, but within certain fixed limits, may be mistress in her own house, as the Provinces to a great extent, but within certain fixed limits are mistresses in theirs....*"

It also described the custom of excluding women from public offices as:

"...*a relic of days more barbarous than ours, but it must be remembered that the necessity of the times often forced on man, customs, which in later years were not necessary.*"

Cairine Reay Wilson, a Liberal, was the first woman to be appointed to the Senate in 1930. The Judicial Committee's jurisdiction over Canada continued until 1933 for criminal appeals and until 1949 for civil appeals.

Years later in 1979, the Canadian Government decided to commemorate the *Persons Case* on the 50th anniversary of the decree by honouring females who had made outstanding contributions to promoting the equality of women.

The Hon. David S. H. MacDonald, P.C., and then Secretary of State, Minister of Communications and Minister Responsible for the Status of Women appointed the Persons Case Award Committee to select recipients for the Governor General's annual Awards in Commemoration of the *Persons Case*.

*"I was asked to recommend the Persons
Award to the Prime Minister by Maureen O'Neil
of the Status of Women Canada to commemorate
the 50th anniversary of the infamous and ground-
breaking Persons Case. Ruth Bell had demonstrated
a lifelong concern for the welfare of people by virtue
of the role and the road she traveled in advancing
the status of women. That is why I asked her to
serve on the initial selection committee for the
Persons Award in 1979."*

The Hon. David S.H. MacDonald, P.C.

As a member of the selection committee from 1979 to 1982 and
again in 1985, I was delighted to serve with: Florence Bird who
was a fellow American, Senator and Chair of the Royal Commission
on the Status of Women in Canada; the Hon. Thérèse Casgrain who
was the first woman to lead a provincial political party in Canada;
Kay Macpherson who founded the peace group Voice of Women
(VOW); and VOW founding member Muriel Duckworth.

The medal, designed by Dora DePedery-Hunt, a sculptress and
a refugee from Hungary, features the images of five women. The
first recipients were:

Dr. Elizabeth Bagshaw, Hamilton, Ontario

The Hon. Thérèse Casgrain, Montréal, Québec

Sophia Dixon, Saskatoon, Saskatchewan

Mary Two-Axe Early, Caughnawaga, Québec

Dr. Grace MacInnis, Vancouver, British Columbia

Marion Royce, Toronto, Ontario

Eileen Tallman-Sufrin, White Rock, British Columbia

Person's Case—1929—L'affaire personne

From apprehension to action

My apprehensiveness, for the position of women and children and particularly girl children, grew out of my personal experience as the child of a poor widow who became a single, working mother—a socially unacceptable phenomenon regardless of circumstance then. Married women just didn't work outside the home. Social safety nets were virtually non-existent during an era rocked by the stock market crash of 1929, and the rigors of day-to-day living during the Great Depression of the 1930s.

The outbreak of World War II in 1939 sent our young and our best soldiers and nurses overseas. Women in the military became a reality with the formation of the Canadian Women's Army Corps, the Canadian Women's Auxiliary Air Force, the Women's Royal Canadian Naval Service, and the Canadian Women's Auxiliary Corps. Our married women worked in Canadian offices, munitions production lines and other factories. When the *war to end all wars* ended in 1945, companies rehired returning veterans and most women, including bank tellers, were sent home to their non-paying jobs.

When I married two weeks after World War II ended, the usual question was: should a new wife work or start a family right away? You didn't do both. If you stayed at home, you didn't "work." In fact, you worked but weren't paid. My parents-in-law were horrified when I went to work in the university library. It just wasn't the thing to do. My husband's salary just covered the rent and food. We could never afford a car. Had I not worked, we wouldn't have had spending money.

Veterans were eligible for educational allowances and low-interest loans, and a 15-year baby boom was launched. With it, came unprecedented housing construction in suburbia.

Few women had been elected to Canadian Parliament. There were no female Cabinet Ministers. Ottawa's great Charlotte Whitton, who was the first female mayor of any national capital in the world, was one of a slightly larger group of women, elected municipally.

Women's employment opportunities were limited further when the Canadian Government enacted legislation in 1947 prohibiting married women from holding federal public service jobs. If they were getting married, they had to quit. Careers, effectively, were closed to married women. The edict had nothing to do with women's credentials, their desire to work or their economic situation. Some women had husbands who suffered with TB or some other disability while others were supporting husbands in school.

That restriction was lifted in 1955 because of pressure by the National Council of Women (NCW) and the Canadian Federation of University Women (CFUW). That was the same year that I joined the University Women's Club of Ottawa and began a half century relationship with it and the CFUW. I had a small hand in advancing the view that women ought to have a choice to stay in their government jobs after they married.

In the 1950s, approximately half the public servants were women and most worked as typists or in other support roles. The Public Service Commission (PSC), comprised of three males, made decisions on policies and advancement. Given the number of females in the public service, the CFUW and the NCW believed it was time to have a woman appointed to the Commission.

We reviewed the qualifications of some very capable women and discussed their potential with others before we met with the PSC Cabinet minister to present our case and our nominees. We worked hard to have the first woman appointed to the Public Service Commission in 1957. Our strategy of educating decision-makers and legislators was working.

For me, the CFUW and its member clubs and the IFUW provided a network and a base for the reforms we needed to bring about equality between men and women. It allowed me the opportunity, as a volunteer, to correct some of the inequities. No one truly can claim individual achievement for the advancement of women. Many were involved in the protracted processes required to create the momentum and achieve the result; some women initiated the actions and others were supporters.

"I met Ruth at a CFUW meeting shortly after she married Dick. She was working on her Masters. We each held many positions and she succeeded me as president of CFUW in Ottawa. I left Ottawa in 1969, so many of her accomplishments were after that time. We have remained friends all these years. We had an interest in antiquing, books and traveling.

"Ruth was always one to have projects in mind and very capable of carrying them out. She is vivacious, fun and has a good sense of humour. She does like her own way, but she does work well."

Peggy Lossing

My personal experience with pension discrimination at a chartered bank was fresh in my mind. I had great empathy for women who encountered difficulties when they lost their public servant husbands through death or divorce. If they divorced, she had no pension entitlement. She would have to go out to work and usually to an inferior job because she had been at home so long that her professional skills were not up-to-date. Most spouses would take out insurance or an annuity, but a poor man couldn't afford those things. In that case, the mother often went to live with her married children—a situation which could become difficult over time.

When a retired public servant died, his widow received half his pension. If she remarried, she lost her entitlement. There was no recognition whatsoever of the fact the woman had stayed at home to raise the children and run the home. My husband, Dick, brought this situation to my attention when he said many Ottawans over the age of 65 were "living in sin" as we used to say. They couldn't afford to get married because she would lose her half of the pension. Until I found kindred spirits in other women's organizations, I worked at becoming well-informed and began to write briefs on civil service pensions.

Our world was changing

The 1960s ushered in the Canadian Bill of Rights, a new flag, the Canada Pension Plan, Neil Armstrong's historic walk on the moon, go-go boots, free love and flowers, the birth control pill, and a relentless focus on changing prevailing attitudes and policies affecting women.

A compendium of issues banded Canadian women together. Minimum wage rates between men and women differed in some provinces; some post-secondary institutions limited the number of women who could register; pregnancy meant a woman no longer held a job or it disappeared when she was on maternity leave; and a husband's earnings and savings were his.

Equal rights for women meant many things. Some saw it as women's liberation. Some saw it as the ability to make choices. Others called it hogwash. The push for a royal commission to examine the obstacles and create opportunities for women was shared by 32 women's groups united by CFUW president Dr. Laura Sabia who eventually forced a showdown with the Federal Government. Laura Sabia was a formidable woman whom I came to know through the CFUW. I recall Laura's sage advice: "When you encounter obstacles, pray to God and She will help you."

Laura was president when the CFUW's *Report on Women University Graduates—Continuing Education and Employment* in 1967 was released. I had the pleasure of being the editor. This exploratory study by the CFUW was commissioned to probe the reasons for the shortage of qualified personnel in Canada and why women graduates were not using their education. The overall objective was "to provide leadership in encouraging women graduates to augment or refresh their academic skills, primarily to enable them to enter or re-enter employment and to work with universities and government to this end."

Laura, CFUW's national president from 1964 to 1967, spearheaded the Committee for the Equality of Women, a coalition of women's groups including the Fédération des femmes du Québec and campaigned for the creation of a Royal Commission on the Status of Women with the support of Federal Cabinet Minister Judy LaMarsh. When the call for the commission went unheeded, Laura threatened a march of two million women on Parliament Hill. Laura couldn't deliver on the threat—at least not in those numbers—but the strategy worked. Prime Minister Lester B. Pearson appointed the commission in 1967 to "inquire into the status of women in Canada and to recommend what steps might be taken by the Federal Government to ensure for women, equal opportunities with men in all aspects of Canadian identity."

Canada was a signatory to the adoption of the Universal Declaration of Human Rights by the United Nations General Assembly in 1948. The Royal Commission adopted the UN's statement that "all human beings are born free and equal in dignity and rights" and embraced four principles:

- women should be free to choose whether or not to take employment outside their homes,

- the care of children is a responsibility to be shared by the mother, the father and society,

- society has a responsibility for women because of pregnancy and child-birth, and special treatment related to maternity will always be necessary, and

- in certain areas, women will, for an interim time, require special treatment to overcome the adverse effects of discriminatory practices.

When the Royal Commission on the Status of Women, headed by Florence Bird, completed its work in 1970, parliamentarians were presented with 167 recommendations affecting the workplace as well as education, health care, housing, economics, national child care, reproductive rights, and immigrant and minority women.

When it became clear to Laura that the Federal Government intended to allow the report to languish indefinitely, Laura met with the coalition of 32 women's organizations to discuss the next step. A new pressure group was formed in 1971 to force the implementation of recommendations focusing on equal opportunity for women. The National Ad hoc Committee on the Status of Women, created in 1971, was renamed the National Action Committee on the Status of Women (NAC). It became apparent that there were now two schools of thought in terms of advocacy: education based on reasoned, factual arguments, and confrontational tactics built on emotion.

The Trudeau government appointed a Minister Responsible for the Status of Women and created the Canadian Advisory Council on the Status of Women. Some things eventually changed. For example, the Unemployment Insurance Act was amended to include maternity leave, the Canadian Labour Code was amended to prohibit dismissal or layoff because of pregnancy, and some minimum wage rates were equalized between men and women.

Some things didn't change. A national day care program was not introduced nor was a guaranteed annual income for the heads of one-parent families. The Commission tried to deal with poverty issues but was silent on violence against women.

Women's groups today are calling for a new Royal Commission on the Status of Women; I believe that is a testament to the success of the first. Some said the first went too far; others said it didn't go far enough. What it did do was show the power of a coalition. I described that power by penning this quotation which I used frequently: *"If ever the world sees a time when women shall come together purely and simply for the benefit and good of mankind, it will be a power such as the world has never known."*

The NAC diligently focused on women's issues in future years. My perspective, gained as vice-president from 1975-1979, is offered later in this story.

Be a "Nice" Girl!

I want to tell you this story because I think it will help some readers understand the attitudes and behaviours facing women during the 1970s, and why International Women's Year—a topic I am going to cover next—was so important.

This "skirmish" began as a personal crusade, separate from the CFUW. We needed to have more women appointed to the board of directors of chartered banks. After all, 50% of banks' customers were women, and women held a large proportion of Canada's financial resources.

My campaign began when I received the Royal Bank of Canada's notice of its annual general meeting in December of 1974. It did not include the names of directors to be elected or those of the proposed auditors, but shareholders were encouraged to sign the proxy card and return it whether or not they expected to attend the meeting. On December 9, I wrote the Executive Vice-President and Chief General Manager Rowland C. Frazee to advise him why I couldn't award my proxy. Not only did I not know who was being nominated, there was no indication that females were among those proposed.

"Surely a goodly proportion of our customers are women? Surely an expression of opinion and a sharing of their experiences in the financial world would be of some benefit to the bank and its operations. Frankly, I resent the paternalistic implications of seeking my proxy to be used in matters, and for persons of whom I have no knowledge."

That prompted a letter a few days later from the Chairman and President W. Earle McLaughlin in which he explained names were not provided with the notice of the meeting because the qualifications had to be "checked up to the very last minute of the annual meeting."

Mr. Frazee telephoned me to discuss the matter. I found the conversation most rewarding and took the opportunity to re-iterate my position in a letter, an extract of which follows.

> *"...Although directors are primarily chosen from the corporate world or related areas of activity, I think it would be worth consideration to appoint one or two people to represent the majority of your customers... I intend to take advantage of our discussion to send you a few names of women who might be considered for appointment to the board of directors. As you know, the CFUW maintains a Roster of Women who are qualified to serve their communities in various ways. Early in the new year, I shall study it carefully and take the liberty of forwarding to you the names of some of the women with their biodata."*

The next evening as I was entering my home, I heard the telephone ringing. Dick was away. The caller identified himself as Earle McLaughlin himself. At first, I was sceptical; I assumed someone was teasing me so I made light of the introduction.

"It's Earle McLaughlin. I am president of The Royal Bank!" he said in exasperation. "I am calling you from Montreal. You have shares and you haven't awarded your proxy. Why don't you be a nice girl and let me exercise your ballot?"

I felt I was being patted on the head. He didn't realize what he had started.

"No," I replied. "I withheld my proxy because no women candidates were nominated to the board and I think each bank should have a few women representing us." I restated the points I made with his vice-president, namely that a goodly proportion of the customers were females. Apart from the fact that there were well-educated, professional women from which to choose, females were very much involved in community participation which was one of the bank's requirements for appointment. I urged him to take advantage of the upcoming International Women's Year (IWY) in 1975 to announce the appointment of qualified women to its board of directors.

Mr. McLaughlin responded by saying the Royal Bank couldn't find qualified women and expounded on his reasons. Candidates had to be: a person of high business and financial expertise and preferably the president of a business corporation of some size; one who was outstanding in his community and province; and one who owned 2,500 Royal Bank shares—the equivalent of $60,000. It was a rhetorical question, but he asked it anyway. "Do you want a token woman appointed?"

I was startled by his response. "If a person has $60,000 worth of your bank shares, then he or she doesn't know much about balanced investments and he or she shouldn't be on your board," I retorted. "Furthermore, one bank has a nun on its board of directors. You can't tell me she owns $60,000 worth of shares. She has taken a pledge of poverty."

He was dumbfounded. I don't know where I got the nerve. Our conversation became heated when I referred to the bank's public relations fiasco in which a commercial, intended to encourage young people to choose a banking career, depicted "Mary" in the traditional role of a teller. That stereotyping generated a great deal of criticism from certain sectors. Before we finished, Earle asked me if I could recommend a woman for the board. I re-iterated the commitment I already made to his vice-president to supply the names of several suitable candidates.

I thought it best to follow-up with a letter the next day to request the specifics of the nomination process and the qualifications of the incumbents. I concluded by suggesting the bank observe IWY. Mr. McLaughlin's response was to send me a list of the board of directors, direct me to the *Financial Post's* Directory of Directors for the directors' background, and report that the Bank was corresponding with the IWY Secretariat.

In the meantime, I persuaded men and women to buy five shares of bank stock which entitled each of them to a proxy vote. We agreed not to exercise the proxies unless a qualified woman candidate was nominated to the board of directors. This wasn't an organized campaign, but I talked to everyone I knew. I had a few bank shares with several banks as did Dick and his friends. Dick was a great supporter of this particular project.

I didn't hear from Mr. McLaughlin so I pursued the issues in a letter to him in March. Mr. McLaughlin cleared up the matter of the number and value of shares a director was required to own as $5,000. In his April letter, my suggestion that the bank participate in conferences to encourage women to pursue non-traditional careers during IWY was described as "interesting." He noted that it might be better for the bank to continue focusing on extensive training for women already employed by the bank to help them advance. He also indicated it was not the bank's custom to elect new directors at the AGM.

It took almost two years to bring this issue to a head. It was Mr. McLaughlin's widely quoted and controversial comments at a bankers' meeting in Winnipeg in the summer of 1976 that created the headlines. The tempest flared up when he said the Royal Bank was unable to find a qualified woman to serve as one of its 48 directors despite a cross-country search. In reality, the bank had rejected a senior insurance executive, an economist and a senior counselor with one of Canada's largest investment firms—women who were recommended by the CFUW. The *Ottawa Citizen* panned the Royal Bank for its "hypocritical claptrap…" in a 1976 editorial, an excerpt of which follows:

> *"If the government and independent research agencies can find competent women to fill key economic posts (Beryl Plumptre, June Menzies, Judith Maxwell and Sylvia Ostry are only a few) then the largest and most profitable bank in the nation can hardly be believed when it claims that its search has borne no fruit.*

> *"Of course, an insight into the attitude of the Royal Bank chief chauvinist can be gleaned from a statement he made when Ruth Bell, past president of the CFUW (and a Royal Bank shareholder) withheld her vote at the annual meeting to protest the exclusion of women from the bank's board.*

> *"Mr. McLaughlin's words were "Be a nice girl."*

The Bank's explanation of why it was unable to find a qualified woman drew the ire of *The Globe & Mail,* and Allan Fotheringham in the *Vancouver Sun* (September 1976). The CFUW, once again, forwarded the names of 15 women to Mr. McLaughlin—economists, chartered accountants, a statistician, a barrister and solicitor, an investment manager, and tax and life insurance specialists. The Ontario Status of Women Council joined in the fray by demanding the Bank's list of directors and qualifications.

Within days, the Bank of Nova Scotia admitted that it too had difficulties finding a woman to sit as one of 26 directors and attributed the issue to the requirement for a person to own 2,500 shares of the bank's stock, estimated at $100,000. The Bank of Montreal and CIBC had women on their boards.

The controversy found its way into the House of Commons when R. Gordon L. Fairweather (MP for Fundy-Royal) introduced a private member's bill on February 25, 1977 to amend the Bank Act's monetary qualifications of bank directors. The section "as it stands is discriminatory to all but a few who can meet the financial requirements and therefore restricts directorships to a small and unrepresentative segment of the population." At the time, the *White Paper on Banking* was under discussion. Included in the proposed legislative changes was the proposal to permit foreign bank subsidiaries to operate within Canadian banking legislation to encourage more competition.

During the course of the debate, Mrs. Simma Holt (MP for Vancouver-Kingsway) noted a recent report on government appointments of women to Crown agencies, committees and commissions revealed that women held only 120 of the 1,162 positions. We really hadn't made much progress since the 1960s.

The Royal Bank eventually appointed a woman to the board of directors. I still spoil my ballot when there aren't any women to choose from, not that I would always choose women because they may not be competent in my estimation. But I want a choice.

In the midst of this, Dick was very supportive of my activities and in some cases, he initiated things through me. As a member of the Ontario Law Reform Commission for more than 20 years, he often tested ideas on me. I remember one particular discussion about women's surnames. Dick was very annoyed that a woman could take her husband's name but a man did not take his wife's name.

Behold the turtle; she makes progress only when she sticks her neck out.

I adopted the turtle as my logo during my tenure as president of the CFUW because of what it represented: Behold the turtle; she makes progress only when she sticks her neck out.

We used the same verve to help shape an environment capable of offering broader educational and career opportunities for women. I encouraged women's organizations to sponsor scholarship programs for older women whose education had been interrupted or terminated as a result of the responsibilities of marriage. Most women either worked or they married and raised the children. An older woman needed enthusiasm, energy and adaptability to succeed at becoming better educated, and she needed support. At the time, there were few opportunities for their continuing education. In earlier days, university evening courses didn't count as university credits and community colleges just didn't exist. Some institutions began to recognize the balancing act most mothers faced. For example, in the early 1960s, the University of Waterloo offered babysitting services as part of its course offerings.

Today, lifelong learning is recognized as fundamental to personal and professional growth. When I returned to Ottawa in 1963 as Ruth Bell, one of the first things I did was to propose the UWC set up a scholarship for mature women who were either changing their career or were returning to study after raising a family. I was particularly proud of one of the recipients—a woman in her late 30s. Her marriage had broken up; she had a couple of kids and her husband refused to support her. She had to find a new career. For three consecutive years, she qualified for the scholarship and went on to become a lawyer.

That being said, I also believed most women had been given more abilities, more talents and more energy than was required in everyday living. I was passionate about women's abilities to contribute to society in politics, in business, in the community, and in the home. I saw women as multi-dimensional. I confess to drawing a line between those women who wanted a choice and those who made excuses for the status quo. Some may not have appreciated a statement attributed to me in a local newspaper in which I said: "Women who just can't get out of a rut or whose husband wouldn't like them to study are suffering from laziness, mental stagnation and downright mental wastefulness." It may have sounded harsh but it was the way I saw it. On the other hand, I believed that change could come about by educating men on the merits of employing qualified women.

The growing number of post World War II baby boomers, who strained the capacities of elementary and secondary schools, now were exerting similar pressure on post-secondary educational institutions. The CFUW recognized universities were expanding but the courses didn't appeal to people who didn't have an interest in philosophical and theoretical discussions, or who couldn't afford the tuition. Many women didn't go to university because a degree did not necessarily lead to a career. As a result, CFUW actively lobbied for the establishment of community colleges in Ontario. We needed to offer another educational choice and venue to ensure students acquired technical skills in a variety of areas. A case in point was the growing reluctance by hospitals to offer schools of nursing. That training would become the responsibility of community colleges. Ontario's decision to build Algonquin College, formerly known as the Eastern Ontario Institute of Technology in Nepean in the 1960s, was an important step for all of the community.

Our local UWC president, Dorothy Bennett Soros, facilitated the process of providing names of female candidates to teach at or serve as head of Algonquin College. At the time, few women were employed by boards of education as principals or in senior administrative staff positions.

We started to make noises by demanding that qualified women be appointed as principals or vice-principals and that others be trained to assume senior level responsibilities in schools. We worked through local school boards and the Ontario Ministry of Education, and lobbied Queens Park to accomplish these objectives. More women are in those positions today.

Finding ways to advance qualified women into positions of responsibility within government and business became a priority. In the late 1960s I participated in a study of Canadian government appointments to boards and commissions in which we discovered less than 70 of 838 possible appointments were filled by women. Our first overture met with the response that not enough qualified women were available. Working with national CFUW president, Dr. Gwendolyn Black, we compiled an initial Roster of Qualified Women consisting of 50 names. We had a CFUW membership of approximately 15,000. The idea of a roster of qualified women was not new. It was introduced in 1946, retreaded in Edmonton in 1969 and re-established in 1970.

As CFUW's incoming national president in 1973, I knew we needed to create a greater awareness of women's potential and we had to expand the roster. After discussing the initiative with two or three Ottawa CFUW friends whose opinions I valued, we decided to pursue the issue with Prime Minister Pierre Trudeau's office. That was followed by a meeting with the Hon. Marc Lalonde, Minister Responsible for the Status of Women. A very sympathetic M. Lalonde authorized a $25,000 grant with the caution that some Ministers regarded political appointments as a perk.

Typically, the incoming CFUW president set up an office within her community because the CFUW did not have a permanent national office. Mine was located within the offices of the Association of Universities and Colleges of Canada. Staff benefits were provided by the Association.

My philosophy can be summed up in three words: *communicate, co-ordinate, consolidate*. I made it a point to visit more than 100 of the 112 UWCs, and to stay in touch with members using 13 newsletters over the course of my term. I adopted a turtle as an icon to accompany my slogan: "Behold the turtle; she makes progress only when she sticks her neck out." The CFUW's annual *Chronicle* and quarterly *Bulletin* were supplemented by five special newsletters, funded by the Federal Government, to promote International Women's Year activities.

With a process and staff in place, we urged all CFUW chapters to recommend qualified members or other women in their communities to serve on government boards and commissions. Many agreed to let their names stand because the time commitment for appointees was not onerous. The names came pouring in—1,500 of them. My husband, Dick, was a big help. He obtained the list of appointments within the purview of each minister. One of my colleagues, Doreen Loosmore, and I called on various Ministers to recommend names and supply credentials. Some of the Ministers were unaware of the scope of appointments within their discretion. Some of the Ministers used it. Others didn't. In the first three years, we achieved one appointment, but I do believe it led the way to opportunities for the many women who now serve at the ambassadorial and deputy minister level. Today, more than 50% of the heads of missions are women. We have come a long way since Canada appointed its first female ambassador in 1958.

About the CFUW

The Canadian Federation of University Women (CFUW), a voluntary, non-profit national organization, has over 10,000 members in 130 clubs across Canada. It is one of 78 affiliates of the International Federation of University Women (IFUW). Both organizations work to raise the social, economic and legal status of women, improve educational opportunities, and create progressive change in the areas of environment, human rights, peace and justice.

The International Federation of University Women held its 1981 conference in Victoria, B.C. In the photo on the left, Jean Simmons of the USA and I listen intently; on the right, Dr. Fumi Takano of Japan and I share a conversation.

CFUW-Ottawa, formed in 1910, is actually older than the CFUW. Earlier attempts to organize a Canada-wide federation of university women were hampered by World War I. Renewed efforts were made because members of the six existing clubs in Ottawa, Toronto, Winnipeg, Regina, Edmonton and Victoria and McGill University alumnae wanted to participate in the first meeting of the International Federation of University Women's (IFUW) meeting in 1920 called to promote international understanding and discourage war. The six clubs met at the Fort Garry Hotel in Winnipeg for the first meeting of the Federation of University Women of Canada in 1919. This federation was renamed CFUW some years later.

The CFUW has pioneered many projects within Canadian communities according to the communities' needs. National committees formed by the CFUW have dealt with many issues. They have encouraged wider vocational choices for women, advocated penal reform as part of a strategy to change attitudes towards criminals, lobbied for academic appointments to universities, performed war work and provided relief aid. Protecting the rights of Aboriginal women, achieving taxation changes and increasing opportunities for women in the public service are just some examples of the other successes. The CFUW also supported the creation of Upper Canada Village as a way to preserve buildings of historical and architectural interests on lands that were to be flooded by the St. Lawrence Power Commission for the St. Lawrence Seaway in the 1950s.

Locally, the Ottawa club encouraged the establishment of a branch of the Elizabeth Fry Society. The School Volunteer Project, initiated by club members, provided teaching support to students with behavioural or other problems. CFUW-Ottawa deals with topical issues of the day—more recently promoting information literacy, advocating for a single national education strategy, and the establishment of a needs-based student financial aid program for graduate and undergraduate students.

The CFUW continues to be a very important part of my life and a springboard for change. I was thrilled to be elected to serve as the president of the Ottawa club from 1968 to 1970, as CFUW's national secretary from 1967 to 1970, as chair of international relations from 1970 to 1973, and as national president from 1973 to 1976. It was an honour to be elected as IFUW's convener of standards from 1974 to 1980, and convener for the status of women and cultural affairs from 1980 to 1986. I was pleased to assist in setting up CFUW-Nepean in 1990 which was chartered in August of 1991, and to serve as the second president for two terms.

---

* The UWC of Ottawa became the Canadian Federation of University Women of Ottawa in 1990.

BE A *"NICE"* GIRL!

International Women's Year:
Pursuing equality for all world citizens

As president of the Canadian Federation of University Women, it was my privilege to encourage our members to mark International Women's Year with three major projects: Foster the Roster, family property law reform and the removal of gender discrimination within the education system. (Ian McCain Photo)

Equality, Development and Peace was the theme of International Women's Year (IWY) in 1975 which was proclaimed by the United Nations (UN) at the General Assembly in 1972. The CFUW saw it as an opportunity to pursue equality of all world citizens—men and women, increase women's participation in local, national and international politics, and encourage advancement of world peace.

Changing traditional attitudes held by men and women, in order to remove limitations on women's human rights in social, political and economic sectors, would have a cost.

The status of women was a growing worldwide issue. In 1974, I led a Canadian delegation of 200 women to the IFUW conference in Kyoto, Japan.

Key resolutions emerging from Kyoto urged participation in International Women's Year, mobilization of the mass media to promote an international development strategy, and greater emphasis and participation in United Nations' agencies to advance women's economic and social issues.

The economic backdrop to IWY in Canada was such that the Federal Government had placed a ceiling on wages and prices in 1975 to curb inflation. Inflation was being fuelled by the 1973 oil embargo and the skyrocketing oil prices demanded by the Organization of Petroleum Exporting Countries. Environmentally, acid rain was an issue.

Reforms to Canadian legislation governing homosexuality, abortion and divorce law were having an impact. More women were entering the workforce. Divorces were increasing. Some people believed a woman's place was in the home and continued to dismiss arguments about women's abilities to contribute to society.

Federally, the Government of Canada established an interdepartmental committee to co-ordinate IWY activities. Some $5 million was allocated to IWY, half of which was assigned to the Office of the Privy Council to be used for advertising and five conferences. The CFUW and the IFUW played a role ultimately in designing the program.

Much was at stake. The CFUW's international counterpart, the IFUW influenced the UN's decision to create IWY. If women were to become more involved in the decision-making process, a new direction would be required. That new direction would support women less privileged and less well-trained by developing in them, as well as in ourselves, a sense of responsibility and an active leadership role. An action program would implement the ideas of equality, development and peace.

As national president, I encouraged members to use IWY as an instrument for social and political change notwithstanding the fact some serious and controversial issues beset the IWY. These were themes I addressed repeatedly in speeches I delivered over the course of IWY—excerpts of which follow.

"We have been charged with negligence, with failure to express the opinion of the CFUW or to offer suggestions; on the other hand, we have also been reprimanded for daring to suggest a course of action to the government and for pushing a practical program for the IWY. We expressed bluntly, our views of the cream puff conferences which would gain headlines for the government and gain nothing for half the citizens of Canada. When we heard of the proposed budget for the conference, we decided they were caviar conferences. We wanted definite, tangible changes and improvements...

"...Let me tell you that we have worked in close co-operation with women's groups across the country and all of us from the traditional established groups such as ours to the way-out groups from radical segments of the community, think alike in this area. The infamous October consultation illustrated to me most forcibly that women can get together to achieve their objectives. We were successful in getting the Women's Program established in Secretary of State and the Minister Responsible for the Status of Women at last has heard us and has revised his program...

"...I dream of our Federation, reaching from east to west, all working together in a course of action, which has been suggested by the United Nations, by the IFUW and by your executive. I would like to see us relinquish, or at least put lower on our list of priorities, our fun groups—gourmet cooking, skiing and flower arranging. Put high on our priorities the actions that will give us all a sense of belonging together."

I urged the CFUW membership to adopt three projects: Foster the Roster at the national level; lobby for family property law reform at the provincial level; and removal of gender stereotyping from all levels and aspects of education at the local level. These were very serious concerns.

CFUW and others such as the NCW and the Business and Professional Women had specific objectives. But some of the general membership had to be coaxed to support those agendas—a message that was mine to deliver to the CFUW.

"At the CFUW level, your national executive agreed last June to push for a concerted course of action. They agreed that every member of the executive should work with her colleagues, and with the clubs in her area—toward a common goal—a course of social and political action consonant with our national purposes.

"Do you want to become a social and political force? Do you want to accept the challenge presented to us by our government? Are you willing to bend your personal objectives to meet those of the greater whole—to contribute to the solidarity of IWY? If the answer is yes, then seek out those in this club and members of our national executive to pursue one of the objectives of this federation for the next two years.

"If you prefer to come to a lecture club, if you prefer to be a receiver rather than a doer, if you wish to enjoy the fruits of your education without assuming the responsibilities, then I would ask you to introduce a resolution to the Council meeting at Victoria next year to dissolve the CFUW, and to save your time and your $4.

"We have the potential for power. In order to realize this potential, we must exercise power with our intelligence, our trained minds, our energies, and our fellowship."

My predecessor, Gwen Black, was very disappointed that our members spent so much time eating and pursuing frivolities and less time on serious work. That happened then and it happens today.

Foster the Roster, family property law reform & elimination of gender stereotyping in education

The CFUW went forward with three major projects during International Women's Year.

Foster the Roster accelerated the promotion of qualified female candidates to senior government and business posts. One anecdotal real-life incident, illustrating the profile of women, took place in an Ontario high school. Grade 12 students were asked to identify all

Here I am with Joan Heyland, on the right, at the CFUW conference in Québec.

the women they could recall from Canadian history. Their collective efforts produced three names: Laura Secord, Jeanne Manse and "Mrs. Sir John A. Macdonald." We urged women across the country to meet with leaders within their communities to convince them to promote qualified women to boards, commissions and executive level positions.

Our list was used by Jean-Luc Pepin when the Wage and Price Control Board was established in 1975. The Minister of Justice Otto Lang was also receptive to our list.

> *"Foster the Roster is an example of the great effort Ruth puts into everything she takes on. She is very articulate and very persuasive.*
>
> *"In an organizational setting, she always projected the image of being very well-prepared and very professional. Her knowledge of process and parliamentary procedures was extraordinary. People learned from her. I have always found her to be very enthusiastic about what other people are doing. She really listens when you are speaking to her."*
>
> *Joan Heyland*

Pressure to reform *family property law* to eradicate serious inequities was fuelled, in part, by the widespread publicity generated by the Murdoch Case. When Irene Murdoch's 25-year marriage to a farmer ended, she had to take her case to the Supreme Court of Canada to obtain an interest in the family ranch she managed and to which she had contributed money from her parents to buy. In 1973, the Supreme Court awarded her $200 a month for maintenance but no interest in the $250,000 ranch because the title was held solely in her husband's name.

I became aware of the need for family property law reform on a personal level. The Bell family property originally extended from approximately the Queensway at Pinecrest and Greenbank Roads to the Ottawa River. In due course, most of the property was sold. Occasionally, Dick would ask me to sign off my dower rights because I had a right to that property. Initially, I didn't know I had that right. So that started it for me.

Married women in Québec couldn't own property. Women in Ontario could, as long as their husbands consented. If a wife inherited property, her husband was entitled to an equal share. If a husband inherited property, the same principle did not apply.

I was not alone. A number of us appeared before the Ontario Law Reform Commission and other bodies to have the family property law changed to make it more equitable—to treat women fairly and justly. The lobby was successful.

Family law reform legislation was enacted in 1978. It built on the Family law Reform Act of 1975 which abolished the common law doctrine "that husband and wife were one person in law—the husband" by creating legal status for married men and women." Finally, men and women were declared to have legal personalities that were separate and distinct from their spouses.

Attorney General for Ontario R. Roy McMurtry described the 1978 legislation in the foreword to the publication *Family Law Reform: Your new rights* as "recognizing marriage as an equal partnership in view of the mutual contribution of the spouses to the welfare of the family, including the previously undervalued contribution of the full-time homemaker. It assures the family shelter by giving special protection to the matrimonial home and assures spouses of an equitable division of their property and possessions in the event that their marriage breaks down. The new legislation removes inequalities which existed under Ontario's old laws of support…The legislation extends the rights and obligations of couples who live in common-law unions and it improves the status of children by abolishing the legal concept of illegitimacy…

However, because no one set of rules can ever be acceptable to everyone, the legislation also provides for the creation of domestic contracts by persons who want to make their own agreements..."

Removal of gender discrimination at all levels and in all aspects of education was our third initiative. Attitudes, inculcated in the early years, carry forward into adulthood and create systemic issues within families and organizations. Adults were encouraged to examine school books to see "is Jane doing exactly what Dick is doing?" We entreated adults to persuade young women to pursue more specialized fields of study such as engineering, science, business administration and economics.

One example was very close to home. When Dick's daughter Judy wanted to go to law school in the late 1950s, Dick thought it would be too rough for her. However, she persisted even though women represented about 20% of the law students. Today, they represent about 60%. In 1986, Judith Miriam Bell was only the third woman to be appointed to the Supreme Court of Ontario since the bench was established in 1875. The first woman to be appointed, Bertha Wilson, went on to be the first woman to sit on the Supreme Court of Canada.

Judy Bell, middle of front row, followed her dream of becoming a lawyer at a time when women represented only 20% of the law students. (Toronto Telegram)

As roles of men and women changed, I believed attitudes would change. We would no longer regard men as strong and aggressive and women as weak and yielding. We would see members of both sexes as whole human beings with individual strengths and weaknesses.

Language began to change. Where once it revolved around male nouns, pronouns and adjectives, a gender-neutral language evolved: fireman became fire fighter, mailman was now a letter carrier, a foreman became a supervisor, a salesman was a sales person, and male nurses became nurses and a lady doctor was a doctor.

More women became bosses—a situation that men had to get used to and other women had to accept.

Employers began to refrain from making statements such as: "I'll have my girl do it" in favour of "I will have my secretary or assistant check that."

Guidelines were issued to writers and editors on the treatment of the sexes to end the practice of describing women by their physical attributes and men by their mental attributes or position. We began to avoid using the pronoun "his" when referring to men and women. Instead of saying, "The average North American drinks his coffee black" we started to say, "The average North American drinks black coffee."

Women did not necessarily take her husband's name as was the custom, not the law. Before Billy Jean King beat Bobby Riggs in three straight sets in the infamous *Battle of the Sexes*—a tennis match televised to 40 million worldwide in 1973, it was Billy Jean and Bobby Riggs. After the match she was known as Billie Jean King. Husbands began to benefit from a situation where they were not the sole breadwinners; husbands did not necessarily pay alimony; and women did not necessarily get custody of the children.

Looking back, IWY was a creation of the United Nations with support from the IFUW—a member of the UN since its formation in 1945. The purpose of IWY was to generate awareness of women's issues. We called them women's issues but they really affected the whole society. People have to be made aware of and sensitized to the issues before they can make a decision to become involved in making changes.

At the 20th triennial in Saskatoon, our report concluded that just 47% of CFUW clubs participated in IWY projects. I was quoted as saying, "The other 53% either think the status of women is not a nice subject for university ladies or are busily engaged in gourmet groups or eating!"

My national successor, unfortunately, didn't hold with the roster effort. I offered to keep the list in Ottawa because that was where the federal lobbying took place. We also used the same list to lobby provincial governments. She moved the responsibility to Regina.

International Women's Day

International Women's Day is celebrated each year on March 8 to commemorate "the day in 1908 when New York City's garment workers marched in the streets to demand an end to the sweatshop conditions that caused the deaths of 128 women in a factory fire. In this tragic incident, the workers of the New York City Triangle Shirtwaist Factory were locked inside the building and when fire broke out, they were trapped inside."

The Hon. Walter F. McLean, Minister of State for Immigration and Minister Responsible for the Status of Women 1986.

The hand that rocks the cradle can and must rock the world

A 1976 poll showed 80% of men would support a woman as an elected leader, whereas less than 65% of women supported women. Many women, especially middle-aged, middle-class women, did not want to rock the boat.

The way I saw it, "The hand that rocks the cradle can and must rock the world!" It was clear that changes in attitude would best be achieved through new or revised legislation and by amending relevant parts of our economic structure.

As a Canadian woman, you stood a much better chance of being poor than a Canadian man. A report from the Canadian Council on Social Development indicated female heads of families were five times more likely to be living below the poverty line than their male counterparts. A male head of the family had 9.3 chances out of 100 of being poor. A woman head, which was the case in more than 25% of families, had a 40.1 chance out of 100 of being poor.

Women earned about half as much as men. Three quarters of all clerical jobs were filled by women but salaries for men in those jobs were 56% higher. In sales jobs where women made up one-third of the workforce, salaries for men were a whopping 168% higher than for women. One survey showed the average earnings for men in managerial jobs was 107.4% higher than for women holding similar jobs.

The National Action Committee on the Status of Women (NAC) began to pressure Statistics Canada to provide a national breakdown of wages for men and women. This was just one of a long list of issues. At the same time, NAC pressed for changes related to human rights, women in broadcasting, amendments to the Social Services Act, support for women with disabilities, and a push for equal pay for work of equal value.

Equal pay for work of equal value was being confused with equal pay for equal work—that is women would receive the same pay as men performing the same job. Equal pay for work of equal value was a far more complex discussion. How do you go about determining the value of a nurse against that of a fighter pilot?

Some women were having second thoughts about the value of legislation because several provinces and the Federal Government already had equal pay laws on the books but the laws were difficult to enforce and not too difficult to circumvent. In one three-year period during the 1970s, only 10 cases of pay discrimination had been investigated in Canada. Laws, originally designed to protect women from employment in unsuitable jobs, merely kept them out of well-paid technical and blue-collar work that was well within their physical and mental competence.

By the late 1970s, the Federal Government passed equal pay for work of equal value which affected its departments, crown corporations and federally regulated agencies such as Bell Canada. A Royal Commission Report on Equality in Employment, conducted by Judge Rosalie Silberman Abella in the mid-1980s, paved the way to a new Employment Equity Act in 1986 but not without some very heated discussions. Some groups maintained legislation was needed to end systemic discrimination fuelled by employer prejudice and social values and to deal with discrimination against women in occupations where there were few men. Business groups argued that supply and demand should dictate wages. Others said higher wages with no marked increase in productivity would drive the cost of Canadian goods and services up, making us less competitive locally and globally. Jobs would be affected. Some felt the number of women employees would be reduced through attrition. The Royal Commission determined that further government intervention through law was required to achieve fairness and justice.

Two Acts were consolidated to create a new Employment Equity Act in 1996: the Employment Equity Act of 1986 which governed private and public sector employers under federal jurisdiction that employ 100 or more employees, and the employment equity provisions of the Financial Administration. An estimated 900,000 employees are covered now. According to Treasury Board of Canada's Secretariat, the Act is intended:

"To achieve equality in the workplace so that no person shall be denied employment opportunities or benefits for reasons unrelated to ability and to…correct the conditions of disadvantage in employment experienced by women, aboriginal people, persons with disabilities and members of visible minorities by giving effect to the principle that employment equity means more than treating persons in the same way but also requires special measures and the accommodation of differences."

It has taken a long time to recognize equal pay for work of equal value because it is complicated and terribly expensive. I know of one recent situation where the lump sum settlement was $125,000. That is a lot for just one employee. There are many others.

Benefits were another issue. My earliest employment experience in the late 1950s with a bank's pension plan was ghastly. I was entitled to "a retirement allowance on good behaviour" while my male colleagues could contribute to a pension. That offensive policy meant I would have nothing to contribute should I move to a new employer's pension plan. In effect, that practice reduced the mobility of the female work force. Banks matched the amount men paid into health coverage and benefits but the same did not apply to women.

Instituting a pension plan was not without its challenges because on the one hand you had management looking at the additional expense of adding approximately half of its employees to a pension plan and on the other, women didn't want to incur deductions because their salaries were so low already. Fortunately, that situation has been improved.

Pension entitlement was quite a different story for the more than 3.5 million Canadian women whose full-time occupation was the care of their families and homes in the 1970s. The long hours, lack of personal wages and entitlement to benefits, and in some cases no financial interest in their home, was further exacerbated by the fact that the value of their work, calculated at $10,000-$12,000 annually, was largely ignored by economists, government and other women. Omitting the value of a housewife's labour from the gross national product excluded the value of goods and services provided by over a third of the Canadian population.

Recognizing homemakers as an integral part of the labour force, we thought, would entitle them to participation in various pension plans. At that time, a widow received half of her husband's pension. If she re-married after being widowed, she lost that pension. If they were divorced, she received nothing.

As the 1970s progressed, we fought for pension changes within the Public Service Commission. We consolidated our approach with other groups. We had representatives from CFUW, the Business and Professional Women, and to a lesser extent, the National Council of Women. We met with the principals of the Public Service Commission (PSC) and the Privy Council.

We were confident because we had dealt successfully with the Federal Government on the appointment of a woman to the PSC; we effectively ended the Federal hiring policy that discriminated against married women; and we prevailed in terminating the policy requiring an estate tax between spouses in 1969.

At the outset, the PSC and Privy Council were dumbfounded by our pension-splitting lobby. We were told it would be terribly complicated, too expensive, and it couldn't be done. So we showed them why it was necessary and how it could be done. It was a matter of education. We achieved our goal. Now, a spouse can claim part of his/her spouse's pension based on the period of time they live together.

What we wanted was the ability for women as well as men to have a choice, with no recriminations for that choice and to be treated fairly and justly. If a woman wanted to stay at home to make a home, so be it. But that choice should not result in a woman being discriminated against by exclusion from pensions and other social securities. If she wanted to work, facilities for childcare needed to be readily available. If the husband wanted to stay at home while his wife pursued her career, he should have that choice. Maternity leave was really parental leave.

Attitudes ingrained in our early years about the roles of men and women had to evolve to reflect contemporary society. Women weren't taking university courses to make their leisure time as housewives more palatable. They were obliged to take them to prepare for the new world of work. Women needed to be encouraged to enter specialized fields, and barriers that stood in the way had to be removed.

In one instance, the CFUW resorted to the courts to have a will changed in Nova Scotia. A scholarship was to be awarded to a male, notwithstanding the fact that a female candidate had the best credentials. The court ruled in favour of the female. As a result of this ruling, CFUW asked Revenue Canada to review the eligibility requirements of our scholarship program. We acted immediately on the advice which was to remove the reference to gender and to promote the program in media targeted at women.

The very complex, emotional and divisive issue of abortion heightened in the 1970s. The question was whether or not to remove abortion from the Criminal Code. There were religious and social ramifications. There were health issues. The women in Canada and other countries permitted themselves to be split, making it possible for political leaders to do nothing. They said, 'You girls (their words, not mine) can't agree.' I would have preferred to concentrate on constructive programs such as encouraging provincial governments to improve family planning programs.

Fellowship at home and abroad

Fellowship is an important part of our organizations. Through the CFUW and the IFUW, we had wonderful experiences getting to know women from other countries at conventions as well as women in our own communities. The 1968 IFUW meeting in Karlsruhe, Germany was no exception. It was there that I met Elizabeth Doe's mother, Olive Dean, who was born in the same village as my mother, and it was there that a program to foster international understanding in Ottawa was engendered.

CFUW's Ottawa's *Diplomatic Hospitality Program* grew out of a warm and animated conversation that took place on a miserable, rainy evening at a hotel in Heidelberg. I was absorbed, completely, by Nancy Radford's fascinating account of how her UWC welcomed and introduced diplomatic wives on their first or second posting to Wellington, New Zealand's capital city. A similar UWC hospitality program existed in Washington, D.C.

Elizabeth Doe and I thought it was a great idea for Ottawa. It would help newcomers enjoy living in the nation's capital and further international under-standing. Canada was coming of age. It had just celebrated its 100th anniversary of Confederation in 1967 by hosting Expo 67 in Montreal which had as its theme *"Man and his World"* and attracted more than 50 million visitors.

A successful meeting was held with representatives of the diplomatic wives, the wives of three external affairs officers and UWC members—Elizabeth Doe, Sonja Lockhart, Edith Eisenhauer and me, although others worked to make this project a reality. That was followed by a well-attended reception for the wives of ambassadors and high commissioners at the Chelsea Club. When we explained our desire to offer hospitality to young women whose husbands were on their first or second posting by helping them with schools, language, health care and hospitals, we received their full support. Elizabeth established connections with External Affairs staff. We entertained small groups in our homes. If they didn't speak our language, we tried to find someone who spoke theirs so they wouldn't feel isolated. Language instruction in English and French was provided by some of our members. We made every effort to help diplomatic wives feel welcome, including the Russians. Eventually, even they joined.

One newcomer lived across the street from me, purely by chance. She didn't know what a snowsuit was until I took her and her little boy shopping. We take it for granted, but how does a woman who normally walks around in beautiful, long cotton dresses or saris know what to wear in the winter? It's all part of learning how to live in a foreign country.

The *Snowshoe Program* for diplomatic wives was an offshoot of the Diplomatic Hospitality Program and continues to be a great way to enjoy the Canadian winter. That idea came to me because I needed more exercise! We often went to Elizabeth Doe's house which was situated at the top of a rise, facing the Jock River and featured a wonderful, long slope. We provided some women with slacks and boots. Elizabeth, and later, Elizabeth Cureton, loaned snowshoes, mukluks, hats, mitts and socks. I will never forget the lady from Brazil. She wore a beautiful fur coat and had a superb hairdo—the like of which you don't see anymore. As she snowshoed down the hill to the river, it was obvious she was having a wretched time. We helped her across the ice and up the other side of the hill. She had had enough. She was going home. Her chauffeur was coming for her. But first, she sat down on one of the snowshoes we had loaned her and slid down the hill. It was so funny.

Ruthie's Snowshoeing Soup, made of consommé, tomato juice, lemon and cloves and served in mugs, was offered as a warmer-upper from time to time.

The weekly snowshoe outings became part of an expanded program of sleigh rides, tours of Parliament Hill, and trips to museums and scenic locations such as Mer Bleu.

Today, more than 300 women from 91 embassies and 75 Canadians take part in the Diplomatic Hospitality Program which culminates in a yearly Christmas lunch I sponsor at the Nepean Sailing Club. When the Cold War ended— symbolized by the demolition in 1989 of the Berlin Wall—and restrictions on freedom were lifted, some diplomatic wives formed university clubs in their own countries.

Our strategy to improve international relations within our multi-national diplomatic community was based on friendship and goodwill.

MATCH and Dr. Norma Walmsley

MATCH was the first organization of its kind in the world. Nobody thought it would work; therefore it was extremely difficult to get the co-operation of government. But thanks to Dr. Norma Walmsley and Suzanne Johnson, women in developing countries actually benefited from this innovative program.

Norma and Suzanne, both of Ottawa, were independent delegates to the first United Nations (UN) Conference for Women in Mexico City—the hallmark event of International Women's Year in 1975 and the launch of the UN's Decade for Women. Most delegates had been selected by their countries to present a particular perspective. That was not the case at Mexico City's unofficial parallel conference called the *Tribune* where 8,000 women delegates, mostly profes- sionals from around the world, openly discussed women's issues.

Clearly, women in developing countries knew what needed to be done but they didn't have the political power to make the necessary decisions. Norma and Suzanne were convinced that change could occur in developing countries at the local level, with some help. They returned, energized by the conviction that once women understood the situation, they would willingly form a support organization. The challenge was to match the talent and skills of Canadian women with the needs of women in less developed countries. It would be the responsibility of women in the developing countries to identify their needs. Norma did not want to send Canadian women to tell developing countries what they needed. I think that is one of the problems, generally-speaking, with international aid today. Organizers have a tendency to send the country what they think it needs which usually differs from what the country thinks it needs.

I was CFUW's national president when Norma briefed me on her plan. Our affiliate, the IFUW was collaborating with the International Soroptimists on similar initiatives to provide advanced training for women in developing countries. CFUW's support was immediate. MATCH International was born thanks to Norma and Suzanne. Norma became the founding president of MATCH International. Her efforts were recognized by a fellowship created in Norma's name by the Norman Patterson School of International Affairs.

I served as founding member of MATCH in 1975, director from 1975 to 1981, and as vice-president from 1981-1983. Mandatory progress reports on the Declaration and Plan of Action drove the agendas at subsequent conferences in Copenhagen in 1980 and in Nairobi in 1985. The most recent conference on Women was held in Beijing in 1995. Success stories in Rwanda, Ecuador and the training centre at Sri Lanka where women learned about sewing, gardening and health and family planning were reported at Copenhagen. One of the students from India, who benefited from the educational support, eventually became the executive-director of MATCH. Here's how Norma recalls the formation.

As a professor of international relations and devel-opment and a member of the board for many non-governmental organizations (NGOs), I had traveled extensively. I had seen how women were doing most of the work in communities where conditions were deplorable. I believed we needed a new organi-zation to bypass government and NGOs and work directly with women. The premise was MATCH would deal directly with women in Asia, Africa and Latin America. For every $1 we raised, the government would be asked to give us $3.

"Women in developing countries would have to identify what they needed, implement it, and be accountable for the results. MATCH would provide the resources—money, strategy

and/or content. I went to the first United Nations (UN) Conference for Women in Mexico City in 1975 as an independent delegate to try out my idea on women from as many countries as possible. I wanted to attend with no strings attached. Few women from developing countries with the exception of wives of government leaders attended but it was obvious women knew what the problems were and what it would take to solve them. What they didn't have was the authority, jurisdiction or responsibility to do anything about these issues. It was evident also that Canadian women needed to be educated on the issues because they had very little knowledge about what was going on in these countries.

"When I returned home, I approached the organizations that had funded the Canadian women delegates including Status of Women and the Canadian delegation for UNESCO—to ask for support to host a post-UN conference meeting in Canada. The purpose was to determine what action should come out of the 1975 event apart from reporting the event in newsletters. I asked for time on the program to present my idea. The national meeting was held and my idea was accepted. I sold $100 memberships to my network of friends whom I had come to know through academic and volunteer circles. Ruth Bell, the president of the Canadian Federation of University Women and a woman who was active in many other organizations, was one of 92 founding members from across Canada and from some international groups *such as the Society for International Development. Eventually, the Federal Government through CIDA agreed to provide $3 for every one dollar raised.*

"Our first projects were quite basic. For example, women in one African community sold their fish, produce and wares at the local crossroads. They wanted a proper cement platform on the ground. Then, they decided they needed a structure to shelter them from the weather. We supplied the $50. The men built it. Gradually, the location became a community centre.

"The abject poverty in India presented other challenges. Education was part of the solution but men would not allow women to participate. There is always a leader. You just need to find the right person in a community to be that leader. Boys were permitted to go to school if they wore the school uniform. Husbands had no objections to women using a sewing centre we set up to enable the women to make the uniforms. While women sewed, they learned about nutrition and other topics. As the knowledge base developed, the voice of women was heard on human rights issues such as violence against women. We marked the 25th anniversary of MATCH in 2001."

Dr. Norma Walmsley

Traditionalists and radicals: Working together

New women's organizations were formed to advance the status of women, and traditional women's groups worked side-by-side with younger and more radical feminists. I worked with Laura Sabia, Maureen McTeer and others to found the Canadian Commission for Learning Opportunities for Women. Its mandate was to address education and training issues affecting girls and women, and to expand their opportunities by creating equity in education and job training.

As a member of the Fundraising Committee from 1974 to 1986 for the Virginia Gildersleeve International Fund, we supported Third World women's education in literacy, science, technology and communications as well as leadership training and community development. Kenya and India were among the countries assisted. One of the seminars I attended to prepare for this work focused on cross-cultural communications. This fund, a charitable and educational fund, was named after one of the founders of the IFUW, Virginia Gildersleeve, who was Dean of Barnard College, the undergraduate women's college at Columbia University, and the first woman delegate to the United Nations.

The United Nations Educational, Scientific and Cultural Organization (UNESCO), which was one of 17 specialized agencies within the United Nations System, came into being in 1947. It sought to build peace based on co-operation and a deep respect for laws, justice, human rights and freedoms. Canada contributed through the Canadian Commission for UNESCO.

From 1976 to 1980, I was invited to sit on the Board of Directors of the Canadian Commission. I soon discovered women, rarely, were appointed to UNESCO. At the time, I was an active IFUW member and the subject of the status of women was a very hot international issue.

The Canadian Commission had a sub-commission on education and another sub-commission on scientific research. With the help of Ambassador Yvon Beaulne and the vice-president of the Canadian Labour Congress, we were successful in establishing a separate sub-commission on the status of women. We had an active role in considering Canadian Government policy on UN-related matters which affected the economic, social and legal interests of women and children. I served this sub-commission as the first Chair from 1976 to 1980. As a life member of the Canadian Commission, I attend meetings whenever I can.

In 1980, I was elected to the first of two terms as Chair of the IFUW's Status of Women and Cultural Affairs Committee which consisted of five members from Canada, New Zealand, Nigeria, the Netherlands, and Japan. You had to be very careful. You didn't do the active things you did in your own country. We ran into obstacles with women of the Muslim faith. One of our colleagues, a very senior officer in Tehran, was assassinated because of her advocacy on women's issues. We worked hard to try to persuade university women in various countries to put a stop to female circumcision—a very serious matter in some Islamic countries and particularly in Africa. We would try to urge our national members to take action or to report issues to us.

Richard Nobbe and I walked along the Mackenzie River at Fort Simpson, Northwest Territories on June 5, 1988 while attending UNESCO's Circumpolar Conference.

Many organizations were becoming sensitized to women's roles and began to take preliminary steps to define internal issues by conducting surveys. Such was the case when I was a director on the YMCA's National Board and head of the Taskforce on the Status of Women. The person with whom I worked was Richard Patten, now a local MPP. He was in charge of personnel and staff matters.

Other new organizations were created. As a founding member of the Canadian Research Institute for the Advancement of Women (CRIAW), I served that organization in 1976 and 1977. CRIAW provided the research needed to probe and report on women's experiences and perspectives.

Ian Morrison, the executive director of the Canadian Association for Adult Education (CAAE) asked me to serve as a member of the Board of Directors from 1977-1979. As a person who was educated as an adult, I was happy to support the CAEE's role: to ensure adults had the opportunity to further academic or technical education.

Women's Legal Education & Action Fund (LEAF) was another non-profit organization formed to promote equality for women and to ensure the rights of women and girls—set out in the Charter of Rights and Freedoms—were upheld in the courts. I was a founding member of LEAF when it was created in 1985.

Over the years, women's organizations have emphasized the contributions of women using a range of tools. The Centennial of the National Council of Women of Canada in 1993 presented one such opportunity. *Women Trailblazers in the Nation's Capital* was the name of a three-hour bus tour of Ottawa and the region which I researched, planned and implemented to mark the occasion.

Using landmarks such as Parliament Hill, the Aviation Museum, the Experimental Farm, RCMP, National Defence, External Affairs and the Supreme Court, I linked the site or building with an historical narrative on a "first" achieved by a woman. There were many firsts from which to choose such as: Margaret Meagher who was the first woman to be appointed to the office of Ambassador; Mary Louise Lynch as the first to be appointed to the National Parole Board; Mary Southin as the first to argue a case before the Supreme Court of Canada; Elsie McGill who designed and tested the Maple Leaf Trainer used to train pilots and during WWII and supervised the production of the Hawker Hurricane fighter planes: Dorothy Downing as the first to organize political campaigns; Grace McGinnis as the first woman to be elected to the House of Commons; Beverley McLachlin, P.C., the first woman Chief Justice; and the Right Hon. Jeanne Sauvé, as the first female Governor General.

"We have been friends through the good times and the bad. I love her dearly but she drives me to distraction. We don't always have the same opinions nor do we do the same things, but we seem to hit it off when we first met through the CFUW. She puts up with my stories about my grandchildren and I put up with her cat stories.

"She was a great protector of society and a leader. I liked to be involved. Through Ruth, I became a member of the local Council of Women and the National Council of Women. We worked on many projects together including archives. Her view was if you were going to do something, you did it well.

You did it better and best before you were finished with it. With Ruth, there was no middle ground.

"I recall one particular instance when the Council of Women was celebrating its 100th anniversary. Ruth planned a tour called Women Trailblazers in the nation's capital to mark the event and I helped her with the details. Ruth did the research and found all kinds of

Here are just some of the members of the Council of Women, Ottawa and area:
From left: Edith Osberg, Sally Roberts, President Ruth Brown, Shirley Browne, Treasurer Mary Maclaren, Maria Neil and Mary Howell

examples of women who had made contributions in public life and in private industry and in various locations in the city. The tour was rehearsed and we drove and timed the route. On the day of the first tour, we had two bus loads of women. I was in one bus. Ruth was in the other. One of the stops was Parliament Hill. We learned that our buses were going to be detoured away from it because of a strike.

When you are part of an organization such as the National Council of Women, you make many new friends.
From left: Pearl Dobson, Sophie Stedman, Ruth, Helen Hnatyshyn and Donna Kumar Heindl.

"I can still see Ruth in her Tilley hat and knee-socks. She got off the bus in a hurry and informed the guard at the gates that he was going to let us through. I thought she might be put in jail. He let us enter. I think ours were the only vehicles allowed on the grounds."

Mary Maclaren

Reflections

When I was a little girl, I was told that if I kissed my elbow, I would become a boy. I tried diligently. I think men have an easier life. They don't have to fight to get ahead unless that's what they want to do.

Where do we go from here? The Canadian status of women in Canada has improved in that there is a recognition that women have as much to contribute to the development of society as men do, but I don't think we have come far enough yet.

Undeniably, biology will always be a factor, a fact proffered by my husband, Dick, when he said, "All the work you and your friends are doing is highly credible, but there is one obstacle that you cannot overcome. Women have to bear the children."

I think it is wishful thinking to believe women can be completely equal to men. However, women can and should expect to be treated fairly and justly. Today, you continue to have different points of view about the role of women. Some are concerned that women are working and running a house, and their husbands are working and doing what they can do which reduces the time they have for their children. Is there enough good family time? You wonder if you have any time for children. The support programs today such as paternity and maternity leave help. However, young people seem to require more material goods than we did.

When I was most active, the status of women was a growing issue in many different countries. Pressure was mounting to treat women as equals. We were creating a new attitude, a new way of looking at things.

There is a movement afoot now for same sex recognition. While the two subjects aren't comparable, in a similar way, women were beginning to emerge. They were entering the workforce. Others thought they should stay at home and raise their children. Now, it seems hard for us to realize that it actually was debated. At that time, except for wartime, the big debate was do I continue to work or give up my career to stay at home and keep house. Some women had university educations. They had ambitions and they had ideas.

I am joined by the Hon. Muriel Fergusson, left and the Hon. Flora MacDonald, centre at a tea hosted by the Speaker of the Senate.

Equal pay for work of equal value was being advanced. Women were being appointed to senior positions in government and often for the first time. It was a stirring time for women. I wouldn't call it turmoil. Women were beginning to raise their heads and make noises and be heard. Some called it conscience-raising.

Some of today's women's organizations say they represent the feminist's perspective. Unfortunately, the word feminist conjures a range of connotations.

When I was active, feminists began to be associated with confrontational advocacy. Generally, they were anti-male and hated men. One of my very good friends will never admit she hates men. But she does. She thinks anything a man does is wrong. She advocates that 50% of appointments to the Canadian Senate must be women and that women must hold 50% of the positions in the Public Service. You may not find that number of qualified people, just as you can't employ a quota system based on race.

If you say you aren't a feminist, some women interpret that as not being on their side. I wouldn't call myself a feminist. I would describe myself as a person working to improve the status of women by bringing about equality. My approach was to persuade and educate. I couldn't have done what I did without the support of my husband. I don't think all men should be thrown out. I kind of like them. I married two of them. My husbands weren't militantly male. When I was married to Bill, the status of women wasn't an issue. It just wasn't a thought. I think, I am all for women, but I am not militant. We had certain projects which I think were legitimate. We worked towards them and we achieved some of them. You are not going to achieve anything, unless you try.

I spoke strongly in favour of what I believed in and what I wanted us to do. I don't think I antagonized my husband, Dick. He was very helpful to me. I think I was firm about issues. But I certainly didn't hate men. I thought the best approach was to use thoughtful, well-presented facts to persuade them on each issue.

CHAPTER FIVE

Investing in the Next Generation

Children are persons too.

Children have rights as persons.

To some people, that may be stating the obvious. But, it wasn't until the1970s that Ontario dealt with the prejudice of illegitimacy by acknowledging children had equal status whether they were born inside or outside of marriage.

That was just one issue. There was much more to do to protect the rights of children—during an era in which the family, as we knew it, was changing. Here's how one report characterized the decision by the federal government to embrace the United Nations' proclamation of 1979 as International Year of the Child (IYC). The family was described as…"a unit bombarded by the forces of the market and shaken by the changes in the status of women, the influence of the mass media, the decentralization of human relationships and other social movements, many of which tend to undermine the family strength and sap its confidence to look after its members, particularly the children."

Organizing Canada's effort was a three-step approach. The Canadian Committee for IYC, of which I was a member, established the Canadian Commission for IYC. Landon Pearson, who was Lester Pearson's daughter-in-law and now a Senator, and I served as joint vice-chairs of the Canadian Commission for IYC. I also chaired the Task Force on the Child and the Law, and the Task Force on Economics and the Child.

The ensuing report: *For Canada's Children: National Agenda for Action*—a blueprint to improve support for children contained a whole range of recommendations. We wanted a secretariat for children's affairs because children's issues crossed jurisdictions of so many federal departments. Child welfare resources required improvements. Income support programs to meet the basic needs of Canadian families needed to be rethought. We wanted the Family Allowance Program to continue, and amendments made to the Income Tax Act to provide child care deductions.

The Commission wanted uniform standards for child daycare centres with financial assistance for exceptional cases, and federally-funded cost-sharing agreements to build and operate non-profit daycare centres.

We proposed parental effectiveness training, parental leave from work for childcare purposes, maternity and paternity benefits, drop-in centres for battered women, alcoholic parents and abused children, more employment opportunities for women and flex-time and job-sharing arrangements with pro-rated benefits.

Our Task Force on Child and the Law advocated children's rights to independent legal representation on guardianship and custody matters and juvenile offences; we wanted more effective ways of enforcing custody orders. We called for laws to protect children from all forms of sexual exploitation, and new young offenders' legislation to replace the Juvenile Delinquents Act.

Eventually, some recommendations were accepted, but not without some agitation on our part.

Amendments were made to the Income Tax Act to improve allowable child care deductions; infant car seats became mandatory; support for shelters for abused women and their children was increased; and new legislation protected native rights of women who married non-native men.

The fragmented structure of federal programs and lack of clear national policy, despite the all-party support for our report, prompted us to call for action in

1981. That led to the formation of a committee for the Implementation of the Recommendations for the IYC Commission in 1982 of which I was a member.

Unfortunately, the National Agenda for Action didn't create the effect we wanted. An issue comes before the public; a commission of an exploratory nature is appointed and nothing substantial is done. That is not to say that commissions are bad. The recommendations are usually well-researched. The Gordon Commission on Canadian Economic Development was an example of a commission that worked. Its reports are still being read. But exploratory commissions don't guarantee legislation will be enacted. It's a way of dealing with controversial issues when the government can't make up its mind on what to do. You dispose of issues by studying them until they die. It is a character-istic of the responsible government system.

It can be discouraging for people who want to contribute. You constantly hope that things might get better. Things will come...gradually.

Youth understanding youth

We did have successes in other areas. I was delighted to be a founder of the Forum for Young Canadians (FYC), a non-profit, non-partisan organization formed in 1975.

Since then, more than 16,000 Canadian high school students have learned how the Canadian government works, in a stimulating, learning environment offered by the FYC. Hopefully, this will be the case for generations.

FYC was incorporated as the *"Foundation for the Study of Processes of Government in Canada."* Its success is due in large part to the continued support of parliamentarians and public servants who take the time to provide tours and host seminars in which students engage in discussions on how government works. Students learn about the responsibilities of citizenship and participate in problem-solving focusing on current issues, all of which leads to a better understanding of democracy and other Canadian points of view.

I recall being asked by Senator Eugene Forsey, to serve on the Board from 1975 to 1981, including two years as president from 1977 to 1979. I worked with Ashbury College's Bill Joyce, businessman Ken Lavery, the former Minister of National Defence the Hon. Leo Cadieux, Joy McLaren and many other keen supporters.

We hosted four, one-week sessions during holiday periods. Each session was attended by 100 to 125 students between the ages of 16 and 18. Canadian high schools were encouraged to nominate two students. In time, quite a few students became pages in Parliament, one or two were elected to Parliament, and several became teachers of political science.

Dick used to say the volunteer work I did for the FYC was the most valuable because it informed and educated young people—the same generation that will lead us in the future—about the Canadian system of government.

I believe in supporting young people, who are making their way in this world, in whatever way possible. The National Arts Centre's *Young Adults Program*, initiated by Pinchas Zukerman, presents an opportunity for young musicians from across Canada and last year, from 20 foreign countries, to come to Ottawa for three weeks to learn from teachers of renown. I had the pleasure of sponsoring two students, a cellist who now attends the Theatre Arts School of New York and a 17-year-old gifted pianist.

Making education accessible

Children and adults are the beneficiaries of the Ontario Educational Communications Authority, more commonly known as TVOntario (TVO), created in 1970 by the Hon. William Davis, Education Minister. Today, TVO fosters lifelong learning opportunities for children and adults using quality educational programming in both languages. On-line resources augment television, and the award-winning children's program has expanded to include programming leading to high school and post-secondary credit courses.

Bill Davis described his visionary concept in 1965 as a "forward step in educational television… taken because our heritage of the past, our knowledge of the present, and our needs for the future must be imparted by all means of communication available…"

I was appointed a director by Order-in-Council from June 10, 1974 to June 30, 1982 by the Hon. James Ault. As Chair of the Compensation Committee and the Human Resources Committee, it was my job to advance qualified women into senior administrative posts and to see that human resource policies were gender-neutral. This was not an onerous task because TVO was a progressive organization. I had the pleasure of working with Chief Executive Officer Ranald Ide who was a well-known educator, and his successor, Jim Parr, a professional engineer.

Five regional advisory councils representing northwest, northeast, southwest, south-central, and eastern Ontario advised the Board of Directors on cultural and educational matters, and promoted programs and services. Subsequently, TVO set up a Francophone Advisory Council and a Native Advisory Council. At the end of my term as director, I served as a member of the

I am shown here with TVO's Elwy Yost and J. Barry Turner (TVO Photo)

Eastern Ontario Regional Council for six years. These regional councils gathered public comment on programming, which at the time, was a unique public consultation technique.

Setting up TVO province-wide was not without its physical or philosophical challenges.

I remember feeling dismayed when a TVO engineer predicted residents living in remote communities in Ontario, eventually, would obtain secondary and post-secondary educational credits via television.

"The day will come when you won't have a teacher. You will sit in front of your television or computer and listen and you'll send your papers to Toronto to be graded," he explained.

"But how will students ask questions and how will the teacher know what his or her students need to know?" I asked. As a teacher, I knew what to stress and what to omit based on students' questions, facial expressions and tone of voice.

Television program content issues in the 1970s generated some lively debates and some very divergent views. The educational value of movies was one example. There were those, like my husband Dick, who saw movies as frivolous entertainment, and those, like me, who argued the educational merits of watching high quality movies. In those days, movies were of first quality and usually had an educational component. When Elwy Yost's *Saturday Night at the Movies* went live on March 30, 1974, who knew the program would become the longest running non-news Canadian television program and that it would become a credit course for York University's Department of Film and Video students?

At one point, TVO produced more French-language educational materials than any other station in Canada and in the world, including France and Québec. Our audience extended into the southern United States.

"You will be interested to know that a good many of the children of Alabama now speak with a Canadian accent!" Ran Ide said in a report about a trip to promote sales of children's educational programs.

I recall one particular incident in which we were interviewing church leaders for their views on the content of a pilot religious program. We invited a Rabbi, a Roman Catholic priest and Bishop Reid, an Anglican. I didn't know Bishop Reid very well but his wife Fran and I went to school together. Our introduction was quite collegial until he asked me what I did.

"Are you the secretary to the president?" Bishop Reid asked.

"No, I am on the board of directors of TVO," I replied.

"Oh, no, no, you must be staff," he said, "You couldn't be on the board. You are a woman."

He said that to the wrong person, so I educated him. That was sort of fun.

Dick, Ruth & Judy Bell Lecture Series

Dick shared my desire to support and educate young people. He had strong ties to Carleton University, having served the Board of Governors and executive committees from 1974 to 1983. He was commended for his "….dedication and enthusiasm and an outstanding conviction in the excellence of the academic endeavours of the University." Dick was very uneasy about students' limited study of Canadian history and Canadian culture. He believed a more stimulating medium was needed to encourage students' and scholars' interest in Canadian studies. That's why Dick made a provision in his will to sponsor an annual lecture on Canadian public and political affairs at Carleton.

I took steps to initiate the series immediately after his death. I was afraid that if I waited, some of our leaders who have spent their lives in politics and public affairs would take this precious insight to their graves. The lecture series was renamed the Dick, Ruth & Judy Bell Lecture Series at my request, following Judy's death to widen the field of interest to include the judicial system, and to recognize her public service as a Supreme Court of Ontario Justice. Judy also was a member of Carleton's Board of Gavernors.

We have just hosted the 12th annual lecture. The series has featured the Right Hon. Robert Stanfield, P.C., the Hon. Joe Ghiz, Mary May Simon, the Right Hon. Joe Clark, P.C., Dalton Camp, the Hon. Flora MacDonald P.C., Hugh Segal, the Right Hon. Kim Campbell, the Right Hon. Chief Justice Beverley McLachlin, P.C, the Hon. Roy Romanow, the Hon. N. Lloyd Axworthy, and Assembly of First Nations National Chief Phil Fontaine.

CHAPTER SIX

Seeing the World
Through Other Countries

"Teddy Cooper"—a beautiful, dark brown teddy bear—joined the family when Roy was a small boy in Cheboygan, Mich. When Roy grew up and lived in Detroit, Teddy stayed with Grandma and Grandpa Cooper until Roy's tiny daughter Ruth went to Flint, Michigan to visit them. She and Teddy fell in love and lived together happily every since. Teddy is a world traveler. He has been around the world in a freighter. He and Ruth got seasick. He has lived in New York, New Orleans, Canberra, Australia and several cities in Canada. He and Ruth went to several universities in three countries. He was very popular with the students. Teddy has retired in Ottawa and Nepean. He and Ruth married Dick Bell and lived in an old house for 30 years. Now he lives in a condo with his old Australian friend Koala and two cats, Fred and Cassie and old Ruth is here too. Teddy enjoys visiting the Nepean Museum which he has done several times to see his long-time bearish friends. Teddy now lives in an old rocker. Despite his mashed nose and broken leg (after all, he is more than 100 years-old), he oversees family activities.

I developed the travel bug early in life, beginning with family excursions during the summer. We traveled by car, primarily in the United States east of the Mississippi, and in Ontario. Naturally, our cars were General Motors products manufactured in Flint, Michigan because that's where Daddy's family lived. Daddy's last car was a Pontiac which we called "the Chief" because it had a little water capsule of Chief Pontiac's head. After Daddy died, Mother had an accident and the car was destroyed. Mother could never afford another one, so I didn't learn how to drive until after I married the second time.

I joined the U.S. Consulate General in Toronto expecting travel opportunities but quickly discovered women weren't officers and only officers traveled. The more stories I heard as I interviewed nationals from other countries who were applying for visas, the more intriguing traveling and exploring different cultures became. With that in mind, I joined Pan American World Airways to instruct staff on customs and immigration regulations that applied to freight and people entering the USA, but my travel aspirations were tempered temporarily by WW II.

The trip with my husband Bill on a freighter to Australia in 1952, which I recounted earlier, was my first major voyage. I wouldn't travel again until 1957 when I visited Portugal, Spain and Italy. In 1960, the Charpentiers, who had helped me through Bill's death, invited me to visit them at their newest post. That gave me the chance to travel to Greece, Turkey, Lebanon, Syria and Israel.

Dick and I loved to travel, so much so that a friendly quip from his daughter Judy couldn't help but make us smile. "I don't know what you have done to my father. Mother could never get him to take any trips at all because he traveled so much with his work, that he was just glad to be at home. Since he has married you, you have taken all these wonderful trips."

Hell-bent for Election is a trip we took in 1965 which I have described to you earlier.

En route to the Commonwealth Law Society's New Delhi conference where Dick was leading a discussion group in 1971, we visited Greece, Istanbul, Turkey and Iran's cities of Tehran, Isfahan, Shiraz the city of poets and roses, and Percepolis. I spent part of the week in New Delhi in a hospital with some type of bug. Once recovered, we visited the Taj Mahal and Calcutta. I found the poverty in India more than I could take. It was appalling. South America had some terrible shacks, but in Calcutta, you walked over people lying on the sidewalk. At one point, we were taken on a bus to do some shopping. As we were about to dismount, starving children ran to the windows and began begging. We were told not to give them anything because it wasn't going to help them. When I came out of one shop, two little children spilled some type of white liquid on my shoes. I was rather stunned. Our hostess scolded the children and cleaned off my shoe. The children had caused the "accident" in the hopes that I would ask them to clean my shoe and pay them for doing it. The poverty was heartbreaking. I felt so inadequate.

We decided to tour South America in 1972 for the first time. We flew from Florida to Guayaquil before traveling to Quito, the capital of Ecuador where I experienced an unforgettable moment. I stood at the

I thoroughly enjoyed my tour of the Middle East, including a stop at Baalbec, Lebanon, in 1960.

Equator with one foot in the northern hemisphere and the other in the southern hemisphere. We went to Lima where we visited the first secretary of the Canadian Embassy Jean Charpentier; Jean was the brother of Georges Charpentier. After Lima, we toured the northern Andes and visited Cuzco— the capital of the Inca Empire and Machu Picchu. We proceeded to Santiago and Puerto Montt, Chile. Three boats and four buses were required to cross the Andes to reach Bariloche, Argentina—a prime ski area. Earlier in the trip, one of my friends and I came down with Montezuma's revenge. Dick and several of his friends came down with it en route to Bariloche. Dick often referred to that trip "as crossing the Andes from john to john." As he boarded each boat, his first task was to find the washroom! From Bariloche, we traveled to Buenos Aires.

We saw the most marvellous waterfalls in the world: Iguaçu Falls (Great Water) located on the borders of Paraguay, Uruguay and southern Brazil. Noted for its breadth of 2.5 miles, Iguaçu Falls was declared to be a natural heritage of mankind by UNESCO in the 1980s. Our next stop was Sao Paulo before going to Brasilia, a planned city capital which was of great interest to Dick. Brasilia was designed and constructed with the express purpose of creating an urban master plan for a capital city. Our last stop was Rio de Janeiro before we flew to New York.

We met with some students on our visit to the University of Wuhan, one of the stops during our five-week tour of China.

Kyoto, Japan was the site of the 1974 International Federation of University Women's (IFUW) conference I attended. As part of that journey, we visited South Korea, Hong Kong, and Manila in the Philippines, Taiwan and Hawaii.

Dick and I toured Tunisia, Egypt, Sudan, Israel and Jordan in 1979.

In 1981, we traveled for five weeks with the Canadian Bar Association to China—a marvellous country. We were treated beautifully. A dinner was held in our honour at the Great Hall of the People in Beijing. We went to Sian—the place of the clay soldiers, Chongquin, down the Yangtze River to Guangxi Zhuang, and on to Shanghai, Penang, Kuala Lumpur, Singapore, Taiwan, Hong Kong and Japan.

In 1983, the IFUW met in Groningen in the northern Netherlands. Following the conference, Dick and I joined an avid group of bell collectors when we boarded the American Bell Association's charter flight in Amsterdam. We flew to Leningrad and on to Moscow, the site of the world's largest bronze bell—the Czar Kolokol measuring 27 feet in diameter. From there, we visited Tajikstan and Uzbekistan and the cities of Bukhara and Tashkent in Central Asia. The Holy City of Bukhara and Tashkent are two of the oldest urban areas in the world. Bukhara is said to have been founded in the 13th century B.C. Its architecture reflects its status as a centre of learning in the Islamic world.

From there, we flew back to Leningrad and on to Helsinki, Finland where we spent a few days with the former ambassador to Canada and his wife Anita Sumelius. We also visited some of my IFUW friends including Dr. Ritva-Liissa Karvetti from nearby Turku, Finland before we flew to Denmark and home.

Dick and I celebrate New Year's Eve at the Kosem Restaurant in Instabul, Turkey in 1970.

I spent at least eight summers attending lectures at Oxford University, Cambridge University and Dublin's Trinity College. Subjects ranged from 18th century English history, King Arthur of the Round Table, and 19th century novelist Jane Austen. After the lectures, our time was our own. I enriched the experience by taking tours and enjoying concerts including several at Europe's oldest concert hall built in 1748—Oxford's Holywell Music Hall.

In 1991, I went with the Canadian Club to Vienna, down the Danube River through Belgrade, Yugoslavia (Belgrade is now the capital of Serbia and Montenegro) and on to Romania and Sofia, Bulgaria. The Adriatic port city of Dubrovnik was intriguing, given its status as an ancient community defined by a pre-sixth century history, and by its role as a merchant marine centre.

I always was glad to come home. A conversation I had with an Intourist guide underlined the freedoms we enjoy in Canada. Dick and I were in Tajikstan, and it was a very hot day. I was sitting under a tree when one of the guides started up a conversation.

"What do you do?" she asked.

"I do volunteer work," I replied.

"What is volunteer work?" she pressed.

I explained various types of volunteerism and my interest and that of my colleagues in advocacy to bring about legislative and social changes.

"We petition the government to do various things with a special emphasis on advancing the rights of women," I replied.

"Oh, we don't need to do that. The government tells us what to do," she replied.

Whether she was accepting of her situation or concerned that the conversation was being monitored, I am not certain.

CHAPTER SEVEN

City of Nepean archives

Volunteerism:
The Politics of Conscience

Some years ago, when I was Dean and a political science lecturer, one of my pleasant duties was to discuss careers and courses with students. Of course, I had sage advice to give as to the careers the trained political scientist or economist could pursue—politics, research, diplomatic service, journalism, and banking. Sometimes my advice was taken. I know of two ambassadors, several university professors, a few advisors to prime ministers, two engineers and several lawyers. But not once, did I think of mentioning the supplementary career of volunteerism.

I began to welcome opportunities to talk about the volunteer as an advocate and the advocate as a volunteer. I had the privilege of giving the address as the first woman speaker to the Ottawa Session of the Bar Admission Course on its call to the Bar on March 25, 1977 at the National Art Centre. The Ottawa and Windsor sessions were a departure from the tradition of hosting the ceremony in Toronto. W. Gibson Gray, of the Law Society of Upper Canada, telephoned me to ask me to be the guest speaker. I remember Dick asking me who was on the telephone. When I told him, Dick said, "No, no, no you shouldn't do that!" He didn't say why, so I agreed to be the speaker.

This was a golden opportunity for me to urge graduating lawyers to place at the disposal of their fellows, their special skills, wisdom and abilities for the improvement of the community, and to help solve some of the social problems of the day.

The power of the volunteer sector in the democratic society cannot be taken for granted. The notion of volunteerism is found for the most part in the western world and more readily established in democratic rather than in strongly centralized forms of government such as dictatorships. In some of our travels, we saw examples of volunteer activity but no signs of advocacy. In fact, in some dictatorships, one of the first acts was to abolish or drastically reduce volunteer activities as occurred to university women in Uganda and in Iran in the 1970s. The presence of voluntary associations is a hallmark of freedom and democracy. They contribute to national unity, international understanding and fellowship.

The face of the volunteer has changed over the years. No longer is volunteer work solely the purview of middle-aged women who have lots of spare time. It is performed by men and women of all ages for many reasons—for the love of humanity, status and recognition, or testing out a new aspect of a career.

There is no reason why we should not be as serious and expert in our life of citizenship as we are in the pursuit of a career. With the rise of urbanization, with the conflicting trends of centralization versus participation, many individuals have encountered increased frustration and marked apathy. Many people have found it essential to discuss social problems and to consider working out possible solutions to these problems.

These social problems and the urge to deal with them produce new leaders and workers who want to participate and to contribute. In the process, they learn more about themselves and discover that they can make a difference.

Advocacy, or the desire to be change-oriented, is an increasingly significant role of volunteers. They are motivated by the discovery that joining forces with others of similar mind and objectives can create change quite often.

Volunteering provides a means of making contact, of restoring individualism, identity and self-respect. Volunteering can provide the means for people to become true participants, not just spectators, in the community's problem-solving tasks.

Over the past years, we have seen a social trend towards the centralization of power and control, most obvious in the governmental sphere of all levels. Called the *"Politics of Power,"* such a focus makes it possible for more universal delivery of services; it also makes for a larger bureaucracy, and the build-up of power tends to lead to tensions.

A countervailing trend is the citizen demand for more involvement. We want our voice to be heard. We want to be part of shaping the decisions regarding the services to be delivered by Big Brother. This might be called the *"Politics of Conscience."*

When a strong voluntary sector is developed to deal with these trends—to balance one and to be a vehicle for the other—citizens have the opportunity to maintain a sense of community. Indeed, the maintenance of democracy may well depend upon the health of the voluntary sector—upon the idea that citizens have a continuing responsibility not only to do things for themselves but also to do things for and with others.

Voting is a way of hoping to have a say about what goes on, of participating in your community. It is often said, if you don't vote, you don't have a right to criticize. Granted, the whole atmosphere around the last few provincial elections and the municipal election has changed. People want certain services from the government and they will vote for the person who will promise to give it to them, whether or not the promise can be kept. We are having a struggle with the costs of social services and health care, and we are having a tough time getting people to exercise their vote. In the autumn of 2003, the Ontario provincial elections were followed closely by the municipal elections. It seems that our citizens were either tired and stayed home or they weren't interested in voting, judging by the 30% turnout in the municipal election. I don't know how you get voters to be more interested because voting is such a fundamental element of our democratic process.

My husband, Dick, once said, "Service to others is where the fun is and is where the satisfactions in life lie. Those who confine their lives to earning their daily bread miss the satisfactions of service to one's fellows. The comfort of the easy chair and TV night after night, or the amusements of night life are not a substitute for the lasting satisfactions of getting out into the community and taking a genuine part in the multitude of decision-making processes which should be made by trained and disciplined minds."

But alas, as I prepared for my *Volunteer as an Advocate* address to the Bar Admission Course, I found myself advocating for another issue. The Ontario Law Society had invited me to a luncheon at the Rideau Club. I had checked my coat and started up the front staircase when the concierge stopped me to say, "Oh no, Madam, I will escort you in the elevator."

"I am going upstairs to a luncheon," I explained.

"Oh no, madam," he replied, "Ladies are not allowed on the upper floor."

"I am the guest of honour at a luncheon here today and I am going up the front stairs," I replied. So I did. He was very upset as he followed me. The old boys, who were reading the papers in the lobby, gave me a long look.

After the luncheon, one of the judges' wives asked me if I knew where the ladies room was. I said yes and we started down the front stairs.

"Oh," she said, "We aren't allowed to go down the front stairs."

"Why not?" I retorted, less than patiently.

"We are women, we can't go down the front stairs," she replied.

"I came up the front stairs and I am going down the front stairs," I replied. She came with me; she was so excited.

That wasn't so long ago; it was 1977.

Recognizing the contribution of volunteers

The definition of volunteerism and the profile of a volunteer have changed in the last 50 or so years. In 1960, the volunteer was usually a women, 40 to 50 years of age, of middle income with lots of spare time. In the late 1970s, the profile of the volunteer was almost equally male and female, between the ages of 20 to 30 or over 60 with an average income of less than $12,000. By the mid 1980s, the volunteer was divided equally between male and female, the largest group was between 25 and 44 years of age, and they spent an average of three hours a week on volunteer work. Most had steady part-time or full-time jobs.

Volunteers and their contributions to the economy, generally, were unrecognized until the National Voluntary Organizations (NVO), a non-profit organization in 1974 formed by Ian Morrison, started to lobby the Federal Government. I was delighted to founding member of NVO, and a director and secretary from 1974-1980. We believed a coalition of groups would be more influential in changing regulations and legislation and in proposing new Federal Government policy governing the voluntary sector, including recognition. The task was accomplished when many voluntary sector groups, motivated by their shared common interests and issues in meeting the social needs of the community, came together. Today, the Federal Government frequently seeks the NVO's advice.

The census was another issue we tackled. It started innocently. One day I sat down to complete a Statistics Canada questionnaire entitled *Highly Qualified Manpower*. In it was a statement that declared "unpaid work at tasks which contributed to the operation of a business or farm owned or operated by a related member of your household should be considered as employment, but volunteer and homemaking activities should not." The next question asked how many hours you worked last week. That made me mad. A quarter of a century earlier, I had pressured Dominion Statistics to track the contributions of the volunteer sector and include it as part of the Gross National Product (GNP).

With help from my NVO colleagues, I was successful in having questions on volunteer work and its value to the GNP added to the census beginning in 1981. In time, the PSC changed its employment form to include a section on volunteer and community service.

I was less successful in having questions added to determine the hours of homemaking and their economic impact. Eventually, Census Canada began to measure time as a resource and included household activities. Not surprisingly, a recent Census Canada survey showed 68% of the unpaid work was done by women regardless of their work in the paid economy. That in itself presents a barrier for women who may want to become more involved in other areas of society.

The Order of Canada and an honourary degree in law

I don't know who nominated me for the Order of Canada, although, I have a suspicion. I was sitting at the dining room table sorting out the mail after our five-week trip to China when the phone rang. It was a caller from Government House which of course was not a surprise because we frequently attended functions there.

"Did you receive a registered letter from us?" the caller asked.

"I don't know, I am just going through the mail now," I replied.

"You have been nominated for the Order of Canada and we want to know if you wish to accept," the caller pressed.

"What?" I said, somewhat incredulously.

"The invitation is in the mail. Do you think you will accept?" she asked.

"I don't know. I do know that you don't appoint enough women. I will let you know!" I responded.

Dick was attending an Ontario Law Reform Commission meeting in Toronto when I reached him by telephone.

"I don't know if I want to accept this because they discriminate against women. They don't appoint enough of them. They need to change their ways," I said.

Judy, Dick and I share a moment at Rideau Hall.

Be A "Nice" Girl!

I was absolutely delighted to receive my insignia of membership in the Order of Canada from Governor General Edward Schreyer. (Photos: Rideau Hall)

"If you can't beat them, join them. See if you can change things from within," Dick countered.

I was presented with my insignia of membership in the Order of Canada by Governor General Edward Schreyer, Chancellor and Principal Companion of the Order, at an Investiture on October 21, 1981. The Governor General presented decorations to two Companions, 24 Officers, 41 members and one Honourary member.

That evening, I had the opportunity to speak with Her Excellency Mrs. Lily Schreyer about the process and the badge.

"This badge is fine for a man's lapel but it isn't very appropriate to pin on a woman's silk dress or blouse," I offered.

"I hadn't thought of that. Thank you for bringing it to my attention," she replied.

By now, you can appreciate that my story is inextricably linked to my husband Dick's.

Dick and I were the first husband and wife team to be awarded honourary degrees together by Carleton University in recognition of our volunteer work.

I was in Switzerland with the International Federation of University Women when Dick called to tell me we had been offered the honorary degrees in law.

"Do you want to accept?" he asked. I was rather stunned.

Before I could mull it over, Dick advised, "I have decided to accept. If you want to accept, you can." He didn't try to influence me because he knew I had questioned the Order of Canada.

Naomi E.S. Griffiths, M.A., Ph.D., presented the Degree of Doctor of Laws, *honoris causa* to Dick and me at Carleton University's 79th Convocation on June 16, 1984. Dick did volunteer work for many organizations including the Canadian Cancer Society and the Queensway Carleton Hospital. I wasn't a lawyer but I had done a lot of volunteer work advocating for changes to improve the status of women.

Excerpt from Citation for Ruth Bell

"…While carrying on a career of university teaching and government service, Ruth has served with dedication and vision at both the national and international level bodies working for university education for women, lifelong educational opportunities for men and women, and organizations striving for the rights of children. She is a role model indeed for the scope and range of her achievements and for the selfless and intelligent activity of her ways.

"It has been said that the last decades have seen people turn from those works that are done for reasons of idealism, from a sense of dedication to the human community, without promise of reward, whether of high reputation or economic goals. Ruth Bell is a living example of those who find joy indeed in work for society itself, the perennial virtue of effort for the public good."

Excerpts from Citation for Richard Albert Bell

"...I have the good fortune of presenting a person whose career has been a living testimony to the old Greek virtue of care for the state. Hannah Arendt wrote in an essay on "Humanity in Dark Times" *that more and more people seem to regard freedom from politics as one of the basic freedoms, a point which, while understandable, leads society to disaster. Humanity to survive must cherish that talent, that friendship for people, which works to make the relationships between individual and community a relationship of honour, of respect, of integrity and of creativity...*

"...His life has been about that crucial question: where is the line between needs and rights of individuals and the demands and necessities of a community? He has always seen that changing circumstances mean the reinterpretation of old statutes, a reinterpretation that must be fashioned in such a way as to guarantee individual freedom and those necessary social bonds. His actions have always betrayed his fundamental belief that humanity is not a disease, a kind of affront to a properly sterile galaxy, but indeed a right and proper species. His speeches have shown a joy in human variety and the essential rightness of human beings...."

We shared the convocation address. Dick presented the *Advocate as a Volunteer* and I presented the *Volunteer as an Advocate*. I stressed the value of volunteerism as a contributor to the economy, to society and to public life.

Putting us to work

In 1998, 25 recipients of the Order of Canada, including me, were invited to bring a citizens' viewpoint to the debate on climate change by participating in the National Forum on Climate Change, sponsored by the National Round Table on the Environment.

We were a group of Canadians from across Canada who had diverse views on climate change from the sceptic to the advocate to those who knew little or nothing about it. Over a period of six days and several months, it was our job to listen to expert testimony and participate in discussions and debates before we recommended a position and how to communicate the issue to Canadians.

This process was set up to deal with the commitment Canada made at the Kyoto Summit on Climate Change in December, 1997, when our federal politicians promised to reduce projected greenhouse gas emissions by 20-25% by 2010.

Dr. Stuart Smith, Chair, began the session by suggesting that while Canadians "support the actions of the government in signing the Kyoto agreement, I don't think it's yet the case that Canadians fully understand the matter. When the going gets a little tougher…there may not be unanimity" on the lifestyle changes and the economics that the protocol might imply. (Summary of Proceedings, February 16-17, Ottawa, Canada)

In our ensuing *Declaration of the National Forum on Climate Change*, we determined that climate change, caused by a build-up of greenhouse gases, could "lead to dramatic changes in sea levels, storm patterns, and average temperatures. Every Canadian has a role to play."

Equally as important, we also determined that action to meet the terms of agreement should be taken only after a thorough economic cost analysis was completed and policies addressing any negative impacts on communities were in place.

The debate focuses on the rate at which climate change is occurring. The natural process of climate change is one in which a portion of the sun's energy is trapped in the atmosphere—known as the greenhouse effect. We are told human activity is accelerating this process.

If not for the naturally-occurring greenhouse effect, experts tell us our average temperatures would be much lower and in fact make the world uninhabitable.

Greenhouse gases, such as carbon monoxide, methane and water vapour in the atmosphere, act like glass and hold the heat inside.

Experts say human activity accounts for generating just four percent of all greenhouse gases. But that's enough to affect temperatures, increasing them by an average of .3 - .6 degrees C. over the past 100 years. A doubling by 2100 could create temperatures that have been associated with major climatic changes such as the last Ice Age, if there is no change in world consumption.

The City of Nepean's Mayor Ben Franklin presented me with the Distinguished Citizen Award in 1982, an honour that I cherish to this day. At left, Mayor Franklin applauds. (Nepean Clarion photo)

Experts also say the level of carbon monoxide has increased by about 30% since the 19th century's Industrial Revolution, largely because of the use of fossil fuels such as coal, oil and natural gas. Clear-cutting of forests is another factor because trees absorb carbon dioxide that would otherwise remain in the atmosphere.

Within the Declaration is a statement that "an effective response to climate change likely will mean higher energy costs for Canadians. Over time, we should all be prepared to adopt energy efficiency measures and increase our reliance on renewable energy. If there is an increase in government revenue from higher energy costs, this revenue must be used to reduce the impact of climate change measures on affected communities, groups and individuals, or to support the development of new energy technologies."

Action steps for citizens ranged from saving energy at home and at work by using cars less, riding bicycles or public transit, recycling materials and reducing consumption of fresh water and other consumables.

Industries would be urged to reduce greenhouse gas emissions and increase their operations' energy-efficiencies.

Municipalities would be encouraged to support public transit, bike paths, funding recycling programs, planting trees, installing energy-efficient lighting, building energy efficiency into local building codes and designing communities to reduce commuting distances.

Federal, provincial and territorial governments were urged to find ways of collaborating on climate change.

The Government of Canada is unlikely to meet its targets without government intervention. If this is done without considering the real impacts and mitigating them, we will be exposed to some critical economic issues. Targeting high energy using industries and one-industry towns—such as pulp and paper, steel, iron and mining—will result in a loss of market share which will affect employment because their costs of doing business will increase while those of their non-conforming competitors will remain stable. That will hamper exports and investment in this country.

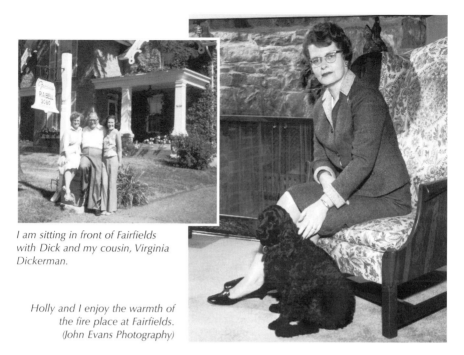

CHAPTER EIGHT

I am sitting in front of Fairfields
with Dick and my cousin, Virginia
Dickerman.

Holly and I enjoy the warmth of
the fire place at Fairfields.
(John Evans Photography)

Fairfields: A Living History

Fairfields, the Bell ancestral homestead on Richmond Road, became my home
following our wedding and honeymoon in 1963. Dick had just been defeated
for the first time in the federal election, and he was returning to his private law
practice. He found the transition difficult because he was so passionate about
public service.

Five generations of Bells resided at *Fairfields*—once known as *Lakeview
Farm*—in the Bells Corners community of Nepean. Three generations were
prosperous dairy farmers and active in politics. One armed Willy Bell (William)
was an innkeeper who ran a tavern from his home. His son, William Nicholson
Bell was Second Deputy Reeve of the Township of Nepean (1890-95). His
grandson, W. Fred Bell was Nepean Councillor (1913-1915), Second Deputy
Reeve (1916-1918), First Deputy Reeve (1919-21), Warden of County Council
(1920), Reeve of Nepean (1922), and Councillor (1929). William's great-
grandson, Dick Bell sold off most of the farm and retained the home in which
Dick, his first wife, Winifred Osbourne Sinclair and their daughter, Judith, resided.

Fairfields has the distinction of being the first to be designated as a heritage property by Nepean's Local Architectural Conservation Advisory Committee: Heritage Nepean on June 24th, 1981.

Heritage Nepean's citation recognized *Fairfields* "as an excellent example of a prosperous Confederation era farmhouse. The two-storey structure is multi-gabled in the Gothic style with excellent bargeboard trim consisting of a series of pendants. Each front gable has ornamental finials. The interior has excellent woodwork typical of the 1870s. The windows, recessed into the two foot thick walls, have paneled window surrounds. This large home is sited graciously on 1.8 acres of the original 600-acre farm holding."

I am going to rely on a presentation Judy Bell made to the Nepean Public Library on the occasion of the City of Nepean's 200th anniversary in 1992 to provide you with some historical information about the Bell family and the homestead. The first official reference to William Bell, an Irish immigrant who was entitled to a land grant, can be found in the assessment rolls of 1823 which listed his holdings as land in the east half of Lot 18, Conc. 2, Ottawa Front. When he arrived, he set about to clear his land and build a scooped-roof shanty. Logs were hollowed out, cut in half and placed on the roof as you would a tile roof. Given the favourable location of his home—located approximately halfway between Bytown and the military settlement in Richmond, William decided to operate a tavern. Two bedrooms upstairs were set aside for travelers, one for men and the other for women. As many as six or seven people slept on the rope bed in each room.

Sometime before 1830, William lost his arm. That didn't affect his ability to operate the tavern which was renamed "One Armed Willy Bell's Scooped-Roof Tavern." The story of what happened is related in a biography of Rev. William Bell of Perth (no relation) written by Elizabeth Shelton.

"On my way home, I called to see a man named Bell of Bells Corners who had met with a shocking accident on the Canal near Hog's Back. When crossing the dam, his horse backed the cart over the dam and they fell 70 feet onto the rocks. The horse was killed. Bell lost an arm and otherwise was dreadfully torn. I saw him several years after, quite well and attending the affairs of his farm as well as the mutilated state of his body would admit."

William and Margaret Argue had eight children. Following Margaret's death in 1843, William married Elizabeth Scrivens. They had four children. Their first son was William Nicholson Bell, from whom this family descends.

Another story, appearing in J.M. Gourlay's *The History of the Ottawa Valley*, *1896* recounts a trip taken by 17 people who traveled in an ox cart on a corduroy road from Bytown en route to Huntley. They reached Bell's tavern at noon. "Mr. Bell was very good to children. He took them out to the garden to pick some fresh onions and Mrs. Bell set a good table at reasonable prices."

The log home was replaced with a stone home sometime between 1837 and 1842 and the 1842 census lists the Bell holdings at 660 acres of which 138 were improved and occupied by the farm. Land holdings included Lot 18 and 19 in Con. 1 & 2, Ottawa Front. The property extended from the Ottawa River to Baseline Road, east of Mosgrove School to the Queensway extension at Richmond Road. William also owned Lot 25 and Lot 26, Conc. 2.

William's son, William Nicholson (WN) Bell married Margaret Elizabeth Hare and they had six or seven children, one of whom was William Frederick (Fred) Bell.

WN's talents as a farmer, who raised prize cows, hogs and horses, were recognized by the Bathhurst District Agricultural Society's Cattle and Grain Show.

Lakeview Farm was almost destroyed when the *Great Fire of 1870* swept through Bells Corners and Carleton County. Dick's father, Fred, who was an infant at the time, was carried by his mother to the Ottawa River where they boarded a boat to Ottawa. They stayed with a relative on Frank Street for approximately one year while their home was rebuilt.

Lakeview Farm was reconstructed utilizing limestone walls from the original building. Stone from a nearby quarry was used to construct a new addition at the back to include what is now the dining room and kitchen. A loft was added to the back of the upstairs to accommodate the hired help at harvest time. The house has been renovated several times since. The semi-circular concrete veranda was re-constructed with pillars, and a bathroom and vestibule were added circa 1910. The house was said to be so cold during the winter that the water used by Dick's mother, Mary Ellen Graham, to wash the floor turned to ice. The house was among the first in the area to be electrified.

The original double parlour was adorned with fret or carved work. It was used only on special occasions—when the rector came to call or for a family funeral. The original floors were made of wide pine planks—some of which you can still see in the basement ceiling. New floors consisting of narrow pine were installed in 1910.

Typically, sleeping quarters were located upstairs. A wall with a door separated the master bedroom from the narrow baby's room. The story goes that when Dick was a little boy, both he and his father became ill during a flu epidemic. Dick's father was sick in bed in the front room and Dick was sick in bed in the baby's room. His mother, who was running back and forth between the two, finally put Dick in bed with his Dad so she could look after both of them.

The small room, used by female travelers who stayed overnight when the house doubled as a tavern and inn, later became a teacher's bedroom. In those days, the school teacher lived in the farm house closest to the school. Dick, his brother Bill who was 10 years older, and Dick's sister Bea who was eight years older, attended school in an old stone building, the site of which now features townhouses. During the winter, Dick traveled to and from school in a sled pulled by his dog. During the day, his dog stayed in front of the stove at the school.

Gerald Parsons, the last teacher to live at *Fairfields*, married Bea. Bill was an engineering graduate from the University of Toronto who worked for Bell Canada. Bill and Bea and their families lived outside of Montreal—one in Beaconsfield and the other in St. Lambert.

Dick's parents used the front room as a family room. In the evening, Dick's mother would rest on a large, leather chaise lounge. His father sat in a comfortable leather chair. The original woodwork around the windows was finished as beautiful natural pine, dating back to 1871.

Some of the land was sold during the Great Depression by William Nicholson and Fred Bell. Lots cost $100 with $10 down and the rest over time. Over the years, the focus on mixed farming changed to dairy by the early 20th century and under Fred's tenure, the farm was recognized as the best kept and best managed farm in Eastern Ontario.

When Dick took over in the 1950s, he renamed Lakeview Farm "*Fairfields*." He converted the front room into the dining room and added a china display case. Today, that room is furnished with Judy's desk and Dick's collection of over 250 bells, many of which I gave to Dick—including a bell used by an English muffin peddler who called out, "Hot muffins for sale," as he walked up the streets. Dick had the fret work removed from the double parlour and a stone fire place installed.

The original kitchen area was used by the housekeeper. Upstairs the hired hand's loft had been converted into a bedroom, sitting room and little bathroom for the housekeeper who was needed when Dick's first wife, Winifred, became ill.

The loft, once used by transient farm hands and earlier in the 19th century as sleeping quarters for male travelers, was converted into a bedroom for the full-time nurse Dick engaged for Winifred. Some of the acreage was sold to pay for treatment Winifred required at the Montreal Neurological Institute. There were no health care plans then. Winifred's death was the second tragedy. Winifred, who had reverted to her maiden name Sinclair, was 10 years older than Dick. Her son, Peter Sinclair, was 15 years of age when he was killed in a bicycle-van collision before the Bells moved to Fairfields. Dick and Winifred's daughter, Judy, was born on February 7, 1940. She was just a baby when Peter died.

When I arrived, our kitchen consisted of a small room—approximately 20' by 6' in size. Originally, it was maiden Aunt Elizabeth's bedroom. In it was a washer, a dryer, a stove, sink and a refrigerator.

We renovated the house in 1968 and restored the dining room to its former glory as a family room; the sitting room became the dining room; a powder room was added; maiden Aunt Elizabeth's room became a utility room; and the original large kitchen was modernized. In the process, we uncovered an archway under the staircase.

As our lifestyle changed, we began to entertain more regularly. Renovations became a priority as a result of an early morning conversation with Dick. It was 7 a.m. and I had five hours of teaching ahead of me that day at Carleton University. Dick said, "Oh, I am having a few people in this evening. Would you put on some refreshments for us?"

"Sure," I replied. "Are cold meats and cheese okay and would you get the beer?

"Fine," he replied.

"How many people—15 to 20?" I asked.

"No, it will be closer to 200," he replied without hesitation.

We had talked about changing things, but we hadn't done anything about it. Here I was confronted with the prospect of entertaining 200 people. I telephoned Arthur Pigott of Morrison Lamothe Inc., a caterer at the time, to explain my predicament. Arthur was prepared to send some coffee, foam cups and enough cold meats and cheese for 100. That afternoon, I set up the tables. The first 100 people who arrived ate; the second hundred didn't!

"You do this to me one more time and I want a bigger kitchen!" I said as I admonished Dick. Plans for renovations began immediately.

When we were renovating, I found a beautiful golden oak bedstead in the basement. It had been painted a bilious green. We had it restored to its original state.

Outdoors, you will find a large, iron school bell. It was the first bell in Dick's collection. When Dick and I traveled, I often visited antique shops to add to my milk glass collection. Dick decided he would collect something—I think out of self-defence. One day en route to Toronto, we stopped at a farm near Belleville to buy a milk glass collectible. Dick was chatting with the farmer when he spotted a large bell. I returned home from Toronto by train and Dick drove back later. When he finally arrived home, he was very, very late.

"What happened?" I asked. "I was getting worried about you."

"Well, I stopped to make a purchase. I bought the bell." His collection featured bells from all over the world including the Russian bear bell I gave him when we celebrated his birthday there. His penchant for collecting bells was obvious. A membership I gave to Dick to the American Bell Association prompted him to start a local chapter. We traveled to meetings in the USSR; Atlanta, Georgia; St. Louis, Missouri; and Hartford, Conn. Even his law firm contributed to his collection. Gracing the wall, inside the vestibule, is a deck bell presented by John Deacon, Jim McInnich, Paul Webber, Walter Baker, David Thompson and Judy Bell.

Fairfields was the site of many political meetings and social gatherings. People liked to come to our house. There was one particular period when we had attended a great many social functions because of my activities in diplomatic hospitality and Dick's position as a Privy Councillor. We wanted to return the hospitality. I suggested we host several cocktail parties.

"A cocktail party tells your friends, 'You are worth one drink to me and that's all.' What's worse, you don't get a chance to talk to your friends," was Dick's reply!

I had a few Sunday afternoon teas which were very pleasant but limited in numbers, so we decided to have a series of dinner parties for 16 people on

Wednesdays because the House wasn't sitting and on Fridays and Saturdays from the middle of October to the middle of December. I developed three menus, had the silver cleaned and the linen washed and ironed.

Bob Stanfield and his wife, Mary, were two of our guests. They were accompanied by two RCMP officers because this was the autumn of 1970 when the Trudeau Government suspended the Canadian Bill of Rights and enacted the War Measures Act to deal with terrorist activities in Québec. The arrival of the RCMP was understandable but unanticipated. I thought, "Where do I seat them? There is no room at the dining table!" So they had coffee in the kitchen.

We had a great time and some very lively conversations with many wonderful guests over the course of the eight weeks. There was one drawback. Dick was very bored with the menu by the middle of December!

Dick, Judy and I shared a love of animals. Before Dick and I were married, Dick came to Waterloo to help me move some of my things, including my cat, to Nepean. Dick had quite a trip because he had to stop several times to let Sandhurst out. Dick had a black spaniel named Holly and a cat called Rastus. The very day Dick was driving back to Ottawa, Rastus was killed on the highway. Sandhurst and Holly didn't care much for each other. But they did co-operate with one another on occasion. Sandy would knock things down for Holly to chew. In one case, Sandy opened a canister of tea and Holly managed to chew up all of the tea bags. Have you ever seen 90 salivated tea bags at 7 a.m.? Sometime later when Sandhurst took sick, I kept him upstairs at the back of the house because it had linoleum flooring. Dick and I took turns giving him medicine every two or three hours. When Holly discovered Sandhurst was sick, she sat with him for several days until he was feeling better. Sandhurst was euthanized in 1975 because he had cancer. A few months later, Holly took sick and died. I went off to Japan to the International Federation of University Women's conference. When I returned, Dick met me at the airport and told me he had a friend in the car.

Dick is shown here with Nicky.

"You will be surprised," he said.

"Does it meow or does it woof?" I asked.

"It woofs," he replied. It was a beautiful Dalmatian we called Nicky. Unfortunately it bit Judy and sometime later, it bit me. Dick was upset by the incidents. Then one morning, Nicky bit him. We gave Nicky away to a farmer where Nicky had room to run.

Preserving our history and heritage

As a family, we had many wonderful memories at *Fairfields* and we were pleased when the City of Nepean gave it a heritage designation. The preservation and restoration of *Fairfields* as a 19th century farmhouse was important to both Dick and Judy. Dick's preference was to have Heritage Canada or Heritage Ontario acquire it but both refused. Fortunately, Judy persuaded the City of Nepean to take *Fairfields* over with an endowment from the Bell Homestead Foundation.

Dick's roots were in Nepean and I grew to know and love the City by becoming involved with Nepean Township and laterally, City of Nepean committees. I had a long history with the Nepean Public Library Board. From 1970 to 1982, I was chair twice and vice-chair for five years. We dealt with a range of issues as the demand for service grew including provision of books in languages other than English. By the end of my term, a third library had been added in Barrhaven. The original library at Rowley Avenue, headed by Chief Librarian Trazsha McDowell had been replaced by the Merivale Road Branch, and a second was located at Bells Corners.

As a member of the Eastern Ontario Regional Library Board from 1977 to 1982, our job was to lobby for funds from various governmental sources and provide peer support to member boards on issues including administrative matters. I was also an executive member and secretary to the Ontario Library Trustees Association from 1978 to 1983. To give you a sense of the issues we were dealing with then, one of my reports dealt with "Computers for Libraries in the 80s." This spring workshop focused on the use of microcomputers, word processors, memory typewriters, Telidon technology and the Ottawa Public Library's new ULISYS Automated Circulation Control System.

Nepean City Council created a special medal in 2000 to thank citizens who worked as community volunteers to improve Nepean s quality of life. I was honoured to receive a medal and accept two others on behalf of Judy and Dick. From left are Councillor Jan Harder, Mayor Mary Pitt, me, Councillor Margaret Rywak and Councillor Merv Sullivan.(Mike Pinder photo)

We had come a long way from using mimeograph machines and manual tracking systems, and clearly the impact of technology was just beginning to be experienced.

I served as a member of the Nepean Archives Committee for two years from 1980 to 1982. I was fervent in my desire to establish a Nepean archives given that its history pre-dated that of the City of Ottawa. My interest grew out of a search I had conducted at the Old Westboro Township Hall in the early 1960s when I was researching material on previous amalgamations for a university paper. Reeve Aubrey Moodie was a great help to me. We got an "A." When I found these very old papers, I felt strongly that they should be preserved. I also believed collecting papers and correspondence of old families was a worthwhile investment. I was perplexed by the fact that there was little information on Fairfields. Dick's response was, "My parents didn't have time to write letters." At the end of my term, the City had a municipal archives but not a community archives. Nepean Museum has taken on the latter to some extent.

Dick was very much involved as a member of the Board of Governors at Carleton University and as one in a group of community activists who worked hard to establish the Queensway Carleton Hospital. There were several attempts before the hospital became a reality, but he, Aubrey and others worked together to a successful conclusion.

Dick and I re-kindled interest in a community museum for Nepean. Dick was determined Nepean's history be preserved and exhibited to show the pioneers' influence on the development of the nation's capital. Indeed, much of present day downtown Ottawa was originally part of Nepean. Dick led the way and I supported him. A meeting at our home, attended by Nepean City Council and MP Bill Tupper, generated renewed interest and the incorporation of the Nepean Museum. Nepean Museum celebrated its 20th anniversary in 2003. I am proud to say I have served on the Board of directors from 1983 to 1985 and from October 1991 to April 22, 1998. I am a life member.

Dick's next objective was to see that Nepean's history was written. That culminated in the writing and publishing of *The City Beyond: A History of Nepean, Birthplace of Canada's Capital 1792-1990* by Bruce S. Elliott. Dick died before the book was finished. It was released in 1992 as part of the City of Nepean's 200th anniversary celebrations and was acclaimed as the best written Ontario local history receiving the Fred Landon Award. Bruce dedicated the book in Dick's memory.

A first for the Bell family

Judy's appointment to the Ontario Bench in 1986 was a proud moment for the Bell family.

Dick and I were absolutely delighted when Judy was appointed to the Ontario Bench in December 1986. The Hon. Ray Hnatyshyn was the Minister of Justice at the time. Judy was only the third woman to be appointed, 110 years after the establishment of the High Courts of Ontario. With less than a month between the announcement and the swearing-in, it was a very hectic time for her. In addition to winding down her legal practice, calling her clients and assigning her work to other lawyers, she had to prepare for the swearing-in ceremony—a very moving occasion. As part of the celebrations, Dick and I arranged a dinner for 50 at Toronto's Albany Club, a strong Conservative Club. Lois Baker, the widow of Dick's law partner, the Hon. Walter Baker, was among the friends and colleagues who attended.

Judy wanted to be a lawyer from the time she was 10 years old. Her father didn't encourage her simply because he thought she would have a very hard time. As a woman, she succeeded in an era when few women were lawyers. Judy was an intellectual lawyer, who had a distinguished academic career at Dalhousie University's Law School in the early 1960s. During her 21 years at Bell, Baker, Judy was an associate and partner specializing in municipal law. Judy also taught at the University of Ottawa, and was active in women's legal associations and the Ontario Bar Association. She always made time to advise young women aspiring to become lawyers. She was dedicated to strengthening women's rights.

When Judy was appointed, the judges generally sat in Toronto. Soon after, they were assigned to move around to various parts of the province—in her case, eastern and northern Ontario. That changed again when judges were assigned to specific regions; she was given eastern Ontario and sat in Ottawa but traveled to Kingston, Belleville and Napanee.

Saying Good-bye

Dick died on March 20, 1988 after an 18-month illness. Prostate cancer metastasized to the bone. He did not want any major medical intervention. I was saddened by the thought that for the third time in my life, I was going to lose a man I loved, to death. Dick's passing was a terrible blow and that awful feeling of loneliness engulfed me once again.

We had a Requiem Eucharist. Peter Coffin, the Rector at Christ Church in Bells Corners, took the service. Many friends including the former Governor General the Right Hon. Roland Michener attended.

City of Nepean staff asked Judy and me to help select a suitable park to commemorate Dick's contributions as a politician, community activist and municipal lawyer. Nepean's Chief Administrative Officer Merv Beckstead and Commissioner of Parks and Recreation Bob Sulpher took us for a drive to view a number of new and existing sites. We suggested Stillwater Park on Acres Road be renamed Dick Bell Park because it was the closest to *Fairfields*.

Two years later, the City of Nepean invited me to open the Dick Bell Sailing Pavilion at the Nepean Sailing Club on Lac Deschenes, part of the Ottawa River. The location of this sailing club on an inter-jurisdictional body of water required Dick, as the solicitor for Nepean, to assemble the property and conduct some intricate negotiations with Québec, Ontario and the Federal Government to arrange the approvals and funding. The 10-year plan to develop this small-craft harbour culminated with the opening of the clubhouse: the Dick Bell Park Sailing Pavilion in 1990 by Mayor Ben Franklin and me.

It was a fitting tribute. I only wish plaques would be erected to tell the story about the people after whom parks and buildings are named.

I stayed at Fairfields until 1994 when I decided to move into a condominium. Judy urged me to get two cats to keep each other company when I wasn't at home. A friend, who heard this, knew of a young family looking for homes for their kittens. They arrived with four kittens in a basket. I wasn't too sure if I really wanted a kitten. Judy had planned to accompany me to the Humane Society to select two cats. Then these came on the scene. I debated and I really couldn't decide. So they rounded up three of the kittens. They

Fred Astaire and Cassandra Jane Austen

couldn't find the fourth, a tabby. The two little boys and I looked high and low, under the beds and in the cupboards, but we couldn't find her. That night, while I was watching the television, out she walked. She had found a hiding place in the back of the television. She had decided to stay. It was July 1994.

Judy was with friends up at the cottage when I called her to tell her about the kitten. They had lots of suggestions for names. One woman suggested "Cassie."

"That's it, Cassandra Jane Austen!" I said. She looked rather like Jane Austen. She had great big eyes. So I called her Cassie for short.

Cassie was very lonely. When I went out, she was obviously unhappy. I asked the family to come back with the three kittens. I looked at the kittens. The smallest one was also the ugliest. It looked like he had a white tie on his chest and his tail and his paws were tipped in white. I made him mine. I had to have a name for him. One day, he jumped up off the couch and leaped up and down and all around, onto the cabinet and over the back of the sofa just the way Fred Astaire used to do. So, that's what I called him. That scrawny kitten has grown into a beautiful cat.

"I remember asking my father earlier in life why he worked so hard for the Church. His reply was, "When I needed the Church, it was there for me. I just want to ensure it is there for the next person.

"My first impression of the UWC in Ottawa was one of intimidation. The executive was formidable. The women sat up on a stage at Elgin Street Public School and called each other Mrs. I remember having to steel my courage before I could speak.

"For some reason, the secretary was often absent so Ruth would ask me to take the minutes. She and I would compare notes at her home after the meeting while my son, Michael, played with Holly, her dog.

"By the time I became president, I had learned how to run a pretty tight ship by watching Ruth lead. My predecessor was her stepdaughter Judy Oyen. Ruth had one basic expectation: carry out your responsibilities to the very best of your abilities. Details were important and there was no shirking. As chance would have it, I worked with her again when she was on the executive of the CFUW and I was the Ottawa representative.

"Ruth and Judy and I became very good friends. We often traveled together and particularly on Easter weekends. One particular Easter, Ruth and I went to Washington, D.C.

We decided to take a daytime bus tour since Judy wasn't due to arrive until later. We completed the tour when the guide announced that Washington at night was a must see. Ruth and I looked at each other and said, "Let's do it." Poor Judy arrived expecting to have her dinner companions waiting for her. I don't know if we were ever forgiven. I earned the nickname "Bus Tour Bagley."

"You know you are compatible when you look at the other person's library and you discover you read the same books or she has books you would like to own. That was the case with Ruth.

"There are many things that Ruth has touched and there are many lives she has touched. Mine is one of them as is that of my son Michael. She is an important person and is very important to me. She is bright, energetic, vitally interested in people including young people, and absolutely prepared to tackle anything. There is no compromise once she has set a course. I hold her in the highest regard."

Junne Bagley

Judy and I were making plans for a trip to mark my 80th birthday when Judy was stricken with an inoperable, virulent form of brain cancer that summer. It was a terrible situation and a shock to all who knew her. She was ill for nine months. One day in October, I received a message. Judy wanted to see me right away.

She and Alastair Speirs, an architect, had decided to marry after a long-term relationship spanning more than a decade. Alastair, who lived in Toronto, traveled back and forth every week to *Fairfields*. When I arrived, he left us alone to discuss the wedding details.

Judy was having difficulty speaking at this stage. She asked me a question but I couldn't understand what she was saying.

"I will do anything you want me to do to help," I said.

She tried again to ask the question.

"May I bring you some dresses from which you can select?" I asked.

"No," she said and tried the question again.

"May I telephone family and friends to invite them to the wedding," I asked.

"No," she said. She was trying so hard to express herself but couldn't.

"I would be happy to arrange the church service for you," I offered.

At this point, she was in great distress but she succeeded in speaking.

"I want….I want….I want you….to be my best woman," she said.

I was touched. Judy and Alastair were married in October 1999.

In November, a group of lawyers and judges, trained by the Great Canada Theatre Company, staged the play *"Twelve Angry Jurors,"* based on the movie *"Twelve Angry Men."* They raised $35,000 for the Ottawa Hospital. A March 14, 2000 *Ottawa Citizen* article quoted Paul Webber, Judy's friend and personal attorney, "At some point the lawyers in Ottawa just said. 'Let's do this for Judy Bell. It just came out of the shock of this summer when Judy was struck down by this thing.'"

Judy died on March 11, 2000. It was a terrible blow. She was held in the highest esteem by the legal community she had served for 35 years, not only for her compassion and thoroughness but for her courageousness. Judy often took cases other judges didn't want and she was an inspiration for other women lawyers in what was once a male-dominated profession. It was Judy who made the precedent-setting ruling in 1993 that a common-law wife was entitled to half of her husband's government pension. The Judith M. Bell Trust Fund was created to fund brain tumour research and palliative care in the Ottawa area. An intimate private service at Fairfields was followed later by a memorial service at the Court House, organized by her judicial friends and attended by hundreds of people. I gave a dinner for about 40 of her friends and family who had been very helpful during her long illness.

"It has not been an easy time for Ruth.

Ruth has taken the ups and downs very well. She is a strong person, a fine person with a nice sense of humour, very capable and very straightforward."

Don Eldon

"Judy and Ruth were friends. They didn't always agree with each other but they cared deeply for one another. Judy's death couldn't have been more of a blow to her if Judy had been her natural-born daughter."

Mary Maclaren

CHAPTER NINE

(John Evans Photography Ltd.)

Pages in Time:
Moments and Memories

Printed words are invaluable and irreplaceable. That may seem silly in this day and age but it worries me that people aren't reading. Literature has the potential to enrich and transform our lives. Instead, people spend their time watching television, using the computer or reading junk e-mail. It just distresses me that they aren't reading good literary compositions.

One of my great losses, now that I am legally blind, is my inability to read my beautiful books that brought me such pleasure. I listen to books-on-tape, but the experience is not the same.

I would like to share some stories behind some of my favourite books. Some of my books carry inscriptions by the author or by a special person in my life, and each is linked inextricably to a treasured moment we shared together. These books are rather like stepping stones in the garden of my life.

When I was very young, Daddy bought me books made out of durable, coated rag-cloth. *Uncle Wiggly* was one of the first. When I was six, he bought me *The*

Wizard of Oz by L. Frank Baum. I loved *The Wizard of Oz*. That was followed by a copy of Hans Christian Andersen's *Fairy Tales*. Elsie Dinsmore's *Motherhood* was a book I bought later in a second-hand book sale because it reminded me of my childhood days in Atlanta.

There is a book belonging to Eileen M. Thomas, 1869 who was my father's mother's sister.

A relatively new biography on General Sherman reminds me of a story Grandma told me about how her uncle, General William Tecumseh Sherman, burned Atlanta to the ground when she was a little girl. General Sherman, the leading Civil War Union Commander, opposed General Thomas "Stonewall" Jackson.

My grandfather, Issac Sherman Cooper, gave me his copy of *The Scarlet Letter* by Nathaniel Hawthorne.

East of the Sun and West of the Moon—a story about fairies, was given to me one Christmas by my Grandpa and Grandma Cooper.

Just before Daddy died, he was reading the first volume of the *Forsyte Saga*, a series of books by John Galsworthy.

My mother gave me Sir Walter Scott's *Kenilworth* in 1932.

My high school beau, David Partridge, thought I would enjoy the humour in *Ferdinand the Bull* by Munroe Leaf. I did!

Some Chinese Ghosts by Lafcadio Hearn was given to me by a beau who wrote: To Ruth—How mutely do I send my loving heart to you and that it may always rest in your hand. Martin, April 1941.

The Works of Thoreau, selected and edited by Henry S. Canby, was given to me by Bill on our honeymoon in Boston—the city where we had had our first date. Bill found this book in a shop in Concord on one of our day trips and penned this message inside: To Princess—With all my love and in memory of a glorious day. Bill, September 13, 1945.

I have kept a few of G.A. Henty's books, collected by my father and Bill, such as *For Name and Fame*, *The Tiger of Mysore*, and *In Times of Peril*. Bill usually had his nose in a history book and I was always trying to get him to do something else. That's why he decided to collect Henty books. We played tennis and golf, but not very seriously.

Bill dedicated his thesis on *Henry Wise Wood of Alberta* to me and supplemented it with a handwritten note: "To my wife who has given generously of her time and energy in the preparation of this manuscript." We worked together for many hours. He talked, and I typed and edited the work.

I came to know Judith Wright, one of Australia's outstanding poets, through her parents. Bill was researching Australian's agrarian political movement which was represented by the Country Party when its president Phillip Wright invited us to his 1,500 square mile sheep station at Armadale, in northern New South Wales. Phillip also had a 3,000 square mile cattle station in western Queensland. I acquired several volumes of Judith's poetry: *The Two Fires*, *Woman to Man, The Moving Image*, and *The Generations of Men*.

Testament of Friendship and Testament of Youth by Vera Britton is one of my favourites just because I like her books.

The Reluctant Pioneer was written by Pearl Packard whom I came to know through the Themis Club in Montreal. She recounts the 900-mile canoe trip undertaken by her grandmother Jane Stone, her husband John McIntyre, and their infant daughter from Lachine, Québec in 1849 to a new northern Ontario post at Hudson Bay.

Politics Canada is a collection of essays on Canadian political affairs published by McGraw-Hill and edited by Paul Fox, a professor of political science at the University of Toronto. It includes a newsletter I wrote on *Electing a Canadian Government in 1962* and an article by one of Judy's friends, François Lemieux. Francois and I used to joke about how we found ourselves together "between the covers" of this book.

Canada Votes, A Handbook of Federal and Provincial Election Data was authored by Howard A. Scarrow, an American Fulbright Scholar who was in Australia when Bill and I were there. We became good friends. When Howard returned to the States, we kept in touch. He came up to Montreal to talk to me about his plans for this book—a commentary and statistical breakdown of federal election results beginning with 1921. Elections prior to 1921 as well as provincial elections also were tabulated. I used the Parliamentary Guides and Elections Canada reports to gather statistics for him. When he finished the writing, I re-checked for him. He included a note: To Ruth with high appreciation for her unbelievable assistance—Howard.

A Woman in a Man's World by Thérèse Casgrain was one I enjoyed. I came to know Thérèse through my work with the Status of Women and the Persons Award Selection Committee.

Nigerian Art: Life in the History of West African Sculpture by Frank Will was given to Dick and me by Ade Oluwasanmi, president of the University of Ife when he had dinner with us at Fairfields. He was married to a Jamaican who was educated in the United States.

Numerous books on bells and milk glass help guide Dick and me in our negotiations for collectibles.

Aunt Dorothy gave me *An Exaltation of Larks* by James Lipton, a book about collective nouns and a folio edition of Jane Austen, an English novelist known for her satirical stories of early 19th century English society. As a school girl, we had studied Jane Austen's *Pride and Prejudice*. I reconnected with Jane Austen's *Pride and Prejudice* when London Little Theatre had a casting call. My audition resulted in a walk-on part as a maid, and an off-stage position as props mistress.

Years later at *Fairfields*, I happened to watch the movie: Jane Austen's *Persuasion*. I enjoyed the film so much that I borrowed all six of her books from the library. That winter while visiting Dorothy Rolph in New York, I told her how I had become re-acquainted with Jane Austen through television. Dorothy was not a fan of television because she believed it was destroying the love of reading, literature and other fine things. That prompted Dorothy to tell me about a story in *New Yorker Magazine* that announced the recent formation of the Jane Austen Society of North America. Shortly after, Dorothy sent me a membership, and a beautiful folio edition of all of Jane Austen's books. It was the beginning of another wonderful journey into Jane's world of literature and many new friendships that spanned decades and more than one continent.

As a devoted fan of Jane Austen's, it was a treat to visit her cottage in Chawton, England.

The Jane Austen Society of North America was founded in the autumn of 1979 by J. David (Jack) Grey, a high school teacher who later became a good friend of mine, Joan Austen-Leigh, a great-niece of Jane Austen who lived in Victoria, B.C., and Henry G. Burke of Baltimore, Maryland. Some time later, the Ottawa chapter was formed by Helen Denman, a Jane Austen devotee. Helen could quote chapter and verse from Jane Austen. Helen was amazing and we became good friends. Dick and I loved to sponsored Jane Austen events at Fairfields. I continue to host an annual Jane Austen birthday at the Chelsea Club on the Sunday closest to her December 16th birthday.

Many of my books deal with the status of women such as *Clear Spirit: Twenty Canadian Women and Their Times* edited by Mary Quale Innis, *The Underside of History: A View of Women through Time* by Dr. Elise Boulding, *Women in Medieval Life* by Margaret Wade Labarge, *Meditations* with Hildegard of Bingen, and *The Unfinished Revolution* by Doris Anderson.

Inside *Eugene Forsey's book Freedom and Order* is an autograph and note— To Ruth Bell: from her old student and admiring friend Eugene Forsey, Feb. 12, 1976. I treasure that. Imagine me having Eugene Forsey as a student! Eugene also included a note in his book, *The Royal Power of Dissolution of Parliament in the British Commonwealth:* In admiration, respect and friendship October 2, 1985.

The *Canadian Journal of Lady Aberdeen* 1893-1898, published by the Champlain Society and edited with an introduction by John T. Saywell, is quite a good piece of Canadian history, and one I have referenced in several of my speeches. The Hon. Ishbel Maria Marjoribanks married John Campbell Gordon, seventh Earl of Aberdeen and Canada's seventh Governor General. The Marchioness of Aberdeen and Temair was said to be the best Governess General, Canada ever had because of her steadfast commitment to social reform in Canada and internationally. I became intrigued by Lady Aberdeen while I was doing research to support the National Council of Women's (NCW) 100th anniversary in Canada.

Lady Aberdeen, with the help of Henrietta Muir of the *Persons Case* fame, founded the National Council of Women in 1893 to improve the conditions of life of women, their families and their communities; Lady Aberdeen also established the Victorian Order of Nurses for Canada in 1897 and May Court of Canada in 1898. She also started the National Home Reading Union in the late 1800s following a tour of western Canada during which she discovered many farm wives had limited access to books. In 1931, it was re-organized into the Canadian Home Reading Union and consisted of 50 to 60 chapters across Canada. I was asked to join in the early 1970s by a friend and served as president in the early 1990s for two or three years. With less than 10 branches of 10 to 15 members in each, it is rather wobbly, but it is still going. Chapters make contributions to Frontier College every year, and some chapters give awards to the CNIB for the promotion of books on tapes. Other chapters provide money to libraries to buy books. Mary MacLaren and I are the archivists.

Worlds of Women—The making of an International Women's Movement by Leila J. Rupp was given to me by Paul Cornell who penned this inscription: "For Ruth, who has laboured in this field, and who has been celebrated and honoured by her nation, for her dedication. With my love, Paul."

Even my cat has a penchant for books. One day, I noticed Cassie walking down the hall when she suddenly stopped to look at a section of my books. Then, she walked to the next section, paused to examine it, and decided to walk on. When she came to my collection of cat books that include: *All Cats Go to Heaven, Of Cats and Men*, and *Thomasina*, she sat down, put out her paw, took out one of the books, and began to turn the pages.

Cassie before I let the cat out of the bag!

CHAPTER TEN

Fred Astaire takes a moment to pose with me.

The Journey Forward

Some 30 years ago, I gave a speech to a Canadian Federation of University Women's audience in Sherbrooke, Québec about the changing roles of men and women. I recall stating that society was in a state of flux—brought on by rapid changes in technology, communications, customs, and lifestyles. Sounds familiar today, doesn't it? I predicted a world in which women would be doing every conceivable job from that of a fighter pilot to zookeeper; a world in which men would be quite capable of cooking a good meal or changing a baby's diaper; a world far different from the one our parents or grandparents experienced; and one that hopefully would be a more humane world, a better world for both men and women.

Our challenge was to broaden women's choices by ending systemic discrimination fuelled by prejudice and values of the day. We tried to change prevailing male standards and women's behaviours through education and legislation. I believe we succeeded in transforming the concrete ceiling many women faced in the first half of the century into a glass ceiling. In fact, hiring practices, pay scales and promotional opportunities for women did improve as we approached the millennium, but not without some males believing that females, aboriginals, minority groups and the disabled were edging them out of jobs. Yet a 2004 National Post headline: *"Wall Street waking up to discrimination"* tells a different story. The story describes the awarding of multi-million dollar out-of-court settlements to women who charged discrimination in promotional practices. At the other end of the spectrum, some women, attempting to pierce the glass ceiling within organizations, opt to strike out on their own because they believe the odds of success as entrepreneurs are more favourable.

We need to see beyond gender to recognize the valuable perspectives each of us brings to the table by focusing on the person's ideas, knowledge and people skills. Men and women can make different choices today. More importantly, they need to strike a balance so that they can live fulfilling lives.

We also need organizations to see their employees as individuals and support their creative ideas. Large government and businesses often try to manage this corporate intelligence by designing hierarchies and processes to filter the flow of information. Unfortunately, this type of management frequently quells the enthusiasm of individuals who once breathed life into their organizations and leads to politically-correct ideologies, targets and goals.

We can create a powerful energy when we are ever needful of the minds of others. Our acceptance of that responsibility implies that we will set aside our own preconceived notions and take the time to really listen, before we consider a response, and create an action. Whether we truly accept or reject that responsibility is at the heart and soul of our Canadian communities.

In many other countries, women continue to experience spousal abuse and discrimination in matters of family, legal and employment law; others suffer at the hands of their tormentors in war-torn countries or are bought and sold and used in prostitution trafficking rings. Their children are destined for a life of poverty. What will our role be in addressing these issues?

Being active and involved has always been my way of being. I don't understand it. I don't know myself as others know me and I am not terribly introspective. I liked being a leader but on the other hand, if you are going to be a leader, you have to have people to follow you. I liked being busy and doing things with people. There were times when I inherited ideas from others and it was my job to work with others to carry them forward. I am a great supporter of networking. I have met many, many people who played different roles at different points in my life. Some entered my life more than once. I have sometimes wondered what would have happened had we met the people we cared for at other points in our life. I am certain, we would be different people because of the life we lived in between.

As octogenarians, my good friend, Paul Cornell, and I have had the great fortune of sharing many conversations and concerts together.

Staying active and interested in what other people are doing keeps you young and involved. I don't take on big projects like I used too but I still enjoy doing things. I am quite pleased when people ask me to help. I try to do my best for them. It invigorates my sense of optimism about the future of our society as we journey forward—where an individual is valued as a person with unique assets and capabilities regardless of race, gender or generation.

Each of us will face situations in our lives and some will be more formidable than others. When we are faced with these character-building moments, will we grow as we reach out to others or will we retreat into ourselves? Will we consider the lessons of the past? Will we be inspired into action or will we vacillate? Will our energy be paralyzed by the angst of uncertainty, or will we be advocates whose interconnected voices overpower the silence of anonymity?

The challenge will always be how we use our power to choose to work together.

All my best.

Ruth M. Bell

CURRICULUM VITAE

Ruth Marion Cooper Rolph Bell, C.M., B.A., M.A., LL.D. (Hon. Causa)

HONOURS

Order of Canada Member, 1981

Doctor of Laws, Honoris Causa, Carleton University, 1984

Distinguished Citizen, City of Nepean, 1982

St. Clement's Gold Award 1990

Governor General's 125th Anniversary Medal 1991

Lieutenant-Governor's 125th Anniversary Medal 1991

Trinity College's Salterrae Society

City of Nepean Millennium Medal 2000

Queen Elizabeth's Golden Jubilee Medal 2002

EDUCATION

Elementary:
North Avenue Presbyterian School, Atlanta, Georgia

Secondary:
St. Clement's School, Toronto, Ontario
  Head Girl and winner of the Powell Memorial Prize, 1938

University:
B.A. Political Economy, University of Toronto, 1955

M.A. Political Science, Carleton University, 1965: Thesis on Conservative Party Leadership Conventions 1927-1956

MARRIAGES

Wm. K. (Bill) Rolph, Ph.D. (deceased) 1945-1953

Hon. R.A. (Dick) Bell, P.C., Q.C., L.S.M., LL.D. (Hon. Causa) (deceased) 1963-1988

Professional Experience

Dr. Brown, Toronto, Receptionist
1938-1939

United States Consulate General,
Toronto, Immigration Clerk
1939-1944

Pan American Airways, New York,
Customs & Immigration Instructor
1944-1945

University of Western Ontario,
London, Ontario, Library Clerk
1945-1947

**New York University's Graduate
School of Retailing**
Admissions Clerk
Secretary to the Dean
1947-1952

**Australian Vice-Chancellors
Committee,** Canberra, Australia,
Acting Executive Director
1952-1954

**Progressive Conservative Party of
Canada**, Ottawa, Economics &
Political Researcher
1955-1957

Clarke Foods, Montreal, Québec,
Secretary to the President 1957

Bank of Montreal Head Office,
Montreal, P.Q., Research Economist
1957-1962

University of Waterloo
Dean of Renison College
Political Science Lecturer
1962-1963

**Carleton University, St. Patrick's
College, Algonquin College**
Lecturer & Seminar Leader
1963-1970 (comparative
federalism, political parties,
comparative ideologies)

Memberships

Canadian Learned Societies
1955-1980

**Canadian Political Science
Association** 1957-1980

Volunteer Advocacy Activities for the Advancement of Women, Children & Youth

INTERNATIONAL

International Federation of University Women

Membership Standards

Member 1974-1977

Convener 1977-1980

Status of Women & Cultural Affairs

Member 1980-1983

Convener 1983-1986

Delegate to conferences at Brisbane 1965, Karlsruhe 1968, Philadelphia 1971, Kyoto 1974, Stirling 1977, Vancouver 1980 & Groningen 1983

> Representative at:
>
> International Association of Universities
>
> United Nations Conference on the Status of Women 1974
>
> UNESCO Seminar in Berkeley, California on Political Activities of Women
>
> UNESCO Seminar on Women's Political Parties

Virginia Gildersleeve International Fund for University Women

Fundraising Committee member to support Third World Women 1974-1986

Match International Centre

Founding member 1975
Director 1976-1983
Vice-president 1981-1983

UNESCO, Canadian Commission

Board of Directors 1976-1980
Member-at-large and life member 1977-present

Sub-Commission on the Status of Women: founding member & first Chair 1976-1980

Jane Austen Society of North America

1980-present

NATIONAL

Canadian Federation of University Women

National Recording Secretary 1967-1970

Chairman of International Relations 1970-1973

National President 1973-1976

International Women's Year 1975

Projects

> Foster the Roster
>
> Family Property Law Reform
>
> Elimination of Gender Stereotyping in Education
>
> Women Trail Blazers Tour of Ottawa

Progressive Conservative Party of Canada

Macdonald-Cartier Library
Initiator & administrator
1964-1970

Member

Volunteer Advocacy Activities for the Advancement of Women, Children & Youth (Cont'd.)

NATIONAL (Cont'd.)

YMCA National Council
Director 1970-1979

Government Relations Chair
1975-1978

Task Force on Status of Women
Chair 1977-1979

National Voluntary Organizations
Representative

Canadian Committee for
International Year of the Child
representative 1978

Canadian Commission for Learning Opportunities for Women
Founding member

National Association of Canadian Clubs
Executive member 1973-1976

National Voluntary Organizations
Founding member, director &
secretary 1974-1980

Canadian Council on Social Development
Member 1975-1977

Forum for Young Canadians
Trustee 1975-1981

President 1977-1979

Life member

National Action Committee on Status of Women
Vice-president 1975-1979

Canadian Research Institute for the Advancement of Women
Founding member 1976-1977

Canadian Association for Adult Education
Director 1977-1979

Canadian Commission for International Year of the Child
Committee to Establish IYC,
member 1977-1978

Commissioner 1979-1980

> Chaired Task Force on the Child
> and the Law

> Chaired Task Force on
> Economics and the Law

Implementation of
Recommendations member 1982

Governor General's Annual Awards in Commemoration of the *Persons Case*
Selection Committee member
1979-82, 1985

Legal Education & Action Fund
Founding member 1985

More about Ruth M. Bell at National Archives

If you are interested in reading more about the work Ruth and her colleagues did to strengthen the status of women, Mrs. Bell has deposited her files at National Archives in Ottawa.

Volunteer Advocacy Activities for the Advancement of Women, Children & Youth (Cont'd.)

NATIONAL (Cont'd.)

National Council of Women

Recording Secretary 1986-1988

National Economic Chair 1991-1992

Task Force on Policy Development 1993-1994

Economics 1992-1993

Legislation 1996-1998

Archivist 1992-1995

Women Trail Blazers Tour of Ottawa

Life Member

Social Sciences and Humanities Research Council

Member 1987-1990

National Round Table on the Environment and the Economy

Forum on Climate Change Member 1998

PROVINCIAL

Ontario Educational Communications Authority (TVOntario)

Director 1974-1982 and Chair of Compensation & Human Resources Committees; Member of Goals & Objectives, Long-Range Planning & Audit Committees

Eastern Ontario Regional Advisory Council 1982-1988

Ontario Library Trustees Association

Executive member & secretary 1978-1983

Eastern Ontario Regional Library Board

Trustee 1977-1982

Chair of Personnel Committee & Finance Committee

Eastern Ontario Archivists Association

Member 1983-present

Ontario Library Association

Archives Committee 1984

Women's Directorate, Government of Ontario

Jobs for Future, Women Training & Technology

Eastern Ontario Chair, 1985

Archivists Association of Ontario

Member 1988-present

LOCAL

Canadian Federation of University Women, Ottawa

(known as University Women's Club, Ottawa until 1990)

Member 1955-present

President 1968-1970

Archivist Emeritus

Volunteer Advocacy Activities for the Advancement of Women, Children & Youth (Cont'd.)

LOCAL (Cont'd.)

English Speaking Union of the Commonwealth
Member Ottawa 1955-present

Founding member & Secretary (Montreal) 1957-1962

Life member

Notre Dame de Grace (Montreal) Community Council
Secretary 1957-1960

YM-YWCA Ottawa
Board of Directors 1965-1975

(Vice-president, Treasurer, Secretary & Chair of International, Constitutional, Nominations and International Fair Committees)

President 1982-1985

Honourary President

Life Member

National Council of Jewish Women
Award Advisor 1966-1967

Canadian Home Reading Union
Member 1970-present

President 1990-1993

Chelsea Club of Ottawa
Board of Directors Member

Nepean Public Library Board
Trustee 1970-1982 including Chair twice & Vice-chair for six years

Trustee 1983-1985

Association of Canadian Clubs
Member 1973-1977

Ottawa Women's Canadian Club
President 1974-1976

Director 1970-1976

Co-ordinator of 75th anniversary celebrations in 1986

Member 1964 to present

Royal Ottawa Hospital Board
Trustee 1977-1979

Nepean Archives
Member 1979-1982

Nepean Museum
Founding member

Trustee 1983-1985; 1991-1998

Life Member

Ottawa Council of Women
President 1985-1988

Vice-president & Chair of Status of Women, Economics, Legislation, Civic Affairs & Resolutions

Life Member

Ottawa Canadian Club
Member

Nepean's Local Architectural Conservation Advisory Committee (Heritage Committee)
Member 1988-1991

Vice-chair 1989

Friends of the Nepean Public Library
First Chair 1989

Nepean Sailing Club
Member

Volunteer Advocacy Activities for the Advancement of Women, Children & Youth (Cont'd.)

LOCAL (Cont'd.)

Friends of the National Gallery

Friends of the Experimental Farm

Canadian Federation of University Women, Nepean
Charter Member 1991
President for two terms

Prayer Book Society of Canada, Ottawa Branch
Executive member 1996-2000

Carleton Condominium Corporation # 72
Secretary, Vice-President, President
1996-2003

National Arts Centre
Donor
Emeritus Circle

Volunteer Archivist
First Chair of the Friends of the Archives for the Anglican Diocese of Ottawa
Archivist for:
Queensway Carleton Hospital Volunteers
National Council of Women of Canada
CFUW
Bronson Home
Council of Women of Ottawa & Area

PUBLISHED WORKS

Editor of *PC House Journal*
1955-1957

Editor of Bank of Montreal's *Business Review* and author of the following newsletters:

Canada s Expanding Universities 1961

Electing a Canadian Government 1962-1972

Electing a President 1960-1972

Fiscal Federalism 1960

Manpower and Employment 1961

Researcher for *Canada Votes* with H.A. Scarrow 1962

Editor of CFUW's *Report on Women University Graduates-Continuing Education and Employment in 1967*

Law Gazette, Spring 1977 *Volunteer as an Advocate*

AWARDS

Gold Medal in Spelling, North Avenue Presbyterian School 1928

Evening Alumni Award for Scholarship, Character & Service to the College at the 120th Commencement at Washington Square College, New York University 1951

Eastern Ontario Library Board Award for Service 1982

TV Ontario for Service as longest serving director 1982

INDEX

About Andrea McCormick

Andrea M. McCormick is a communications professional with over 30 years of experience in the private and municipal sector. *Be a "Nice" Girl!* is her second book. The first, *"Spirit of Nepean"* with D. Aubrey Moodie, was published and successfully marketed in 2003. Andrea's company, Andrea McCormick Communications Inc., is based in White Lake, Ontario.

Photo Credit: Lux Photographic Services Inc.